SPIRITUAL INNOVATION
EXPECTING MORE // SHIFTING REALITY

COLE NeSMITH

SPIRITUAL INNOVATION
EXPECTING MORE // SHIFTING REALITY

Copyright © 2014 by Cole NeSmith

All rights are reserved. No part of this publication may be reproduced, stored in a retrieval system or transmitted in any form or by any means, electronic, mechanical, photocopying, recording or otherwise, without prior permission of the Author.

All scripture quotations, unless otherwise indicated, are taken from the Holy Bible, New International Version®, NIV®. Copyright ©1973, 1978, 1984, 2011 by Biblica, Inc.™ Used by permission of Zondervan. All rights reserved worldwide. www.zondervan.com The "NIV" and "New International Version" are trademarks registered in the United States Patent and Trademark Office by Biblica, Inc.™

This title is also offered as an ebook.
Visit www.colenesmith.com for more information.

SPIRITUAL INNOVATION // ACCOLADES

"Cole helps shift and challenge how we see our relationship with Jesus, focusing on the practical realities of what it means to see heaven on earth. Cole not only talks about faith and creativity, he lives it out in his love for the Church and the world. Read this book, and dream again!"

//Brad Lomenick
Former director of Catalyst, Author of "The Catalyst Leader"

"I thoroughly enjoyed Cole's beautiful and thoughtful examination of the power and necessity of mystery. Spiritual Innovation serves as a wonderful instruction manual for creatives and non-creatives alike, to dare to dream bigger."

//Ryan O'Neal
Sleeping At Last

"Cole's creative approach to what it means to follow Jesus will help shift how you see the world and then propel you into a new level of effectiveness and purpose in your identity and calling."

//Carlos Whittaker
Musician and author of Moment Maker

"When the Church re-embraces our identity as artists and creative people, we will be filled with a new hope for what the world can look like. Spiritual Innovation ushers us into the power of possessing the image of the Creator and what it means for the world. Cole not only talks about faith and creativity, he lives it out in his love for the Church and the world."

//Jeremy Cowart
Photographer and Founder of Help-Portrait and OKDOTHIS

"Listening to Cole think and talk through spiritual innovation is inspiring. With wide eyes Cole leads to beautiful ideas, not settling for the norm, and being more like Jesus...incarnational. Read this with an open heart, open ears, and get ready to see what God is doing and join Him."

//Charlie Hall
Songwriter and Worship Leader

"Cole's fresh look at spiritual innovation is both inspiring and life-giving. Rooted in a revolutionary faith that has withstood the test of time, this book offers a timely reminder and pathway to embrace the future that God has designed for us to enjoy."

//Charles Lee
CEO of Ideation & Author of Good Idea. Now What?

"Cole possesses the heart of both an artist and a pastor. You'll find no better merging of the two as he introduces us to the groundbreaking concept of spiritual innovation."

//Ben Arment
Author of Dream Year

"This book will challenge everything you thought you knew about being a Christian. With intelligence, wit and grace, Cole examines some of the deeply ingrained (and highly protected) beliefs and practices and of the Christian faith and asks a very dangerous—and very necessary—question: why? What would it look like to give ourselves permission to "do faith" differently, to innovate and grow? Whether you're skeptical of Christianity, resistant to Christianity or have been deeply defined by your Christian faith, this book will open you to a God who is bigger, a faith that is stronger and a life more empowered than you could ever dream."

//Allison Vesterfelt
Author of Packing Light: Thoughts on Living Life with Less Baggage

"When there is much to risk, innovation tends to be the first to go. But when we have nothing to lose, innovation becomes central. I believe this book is timely to address the need to risk for the sake of the Gospel again. Just like the New Testament Church. Cole will inspire you and challenge you to that end in this book."

//Tyler Reagin
Executive Director, Catalyst

"Spiritual Innovation resonates in a deep place inside me. I have a hunger for more than just the white American Jesus I've been shown for so long. Cole reminds me that there's more to Christianity than there's still more to discover about Jesus and more to this walk than I could ever imagine."

//Jonathan Malm
Author of "Created for More: 30 Days to Seeing Your World in a New Way" and Editor of Sunday Magazine

"My friend Cole has asked challenging questions at key moments in my life. Perhaps other people were feeling or sensing the same things, but Cole was the one willing to say it out loud. His honesty is what I admire most. This book is much the same - Cole leading the way, wrestling with the possibility of things looking different, willing to ask the questions."

//Jamie Tworkowski
Founder of To Write Love on Her Arms

SPIRITUAL INNOVATION
EXPECTING MORE // SHIFTING REALITY

TABLE OF CONTENTS

AN INTRODUCTION
I MIGHT BE COMPLETELY WRONG BUT...   **11**

CHAPTER ONE
SOMETHING IS MISSING   **21**

CHAPTER TWO
HOW DID WE GET HERE   **39**
OUR INDIVIDUAL NEED FOR CONTROL

CHAPTER THREE
RELIGION AND POLITICS   **63**
OUR COMMUNAL NEED FOR CONTROL

CHAPTER FOUR
BREAKING FREE FROM CONTROL   **85**

CHAPTER FIVE
THE END OF DOOMSDAY THINKING   **103**

CHAPTER SIX
THE WORLD IS GETTING BETTER   **121**

CHAPTER SEVEN
EXPLORE THE POSSIBILITIES   **135**

157 CHAPTER EIGHT
EMBRACE INNOVATION

171 CHAPTER NINE
DISCOVER THE INFINITE GOD

193 CHAPTER TEN
THE POWER OF LANGUAGE

207 CHAPTER ELEVEN
PERMISSION TO CREATE

227 CHAPTER TWELVE
THE KINGDOM COMES

247 AN AFTERWARD
HONOR AND EXCEED

SPIRITUAL INNOVATION // AN INTRODUCTION
I MIGHT BE COMPLETELY WRONG BUT...

SPIRITUAL INNOVATION

"I might be completely wrong, but..."

That's where we'll start because that's the posture with which I want us to approach this book—both me, as the author, and you, as the reader.

I grew up on books with titles like "The Case For Christ" and "Evidence that Demands a Verdict." I loved consuming the things written in those books, showing up in my middle school classes and debating the cold, hard facts... or, at least, the cold, hard facts as I knew them to be.

All this information gathering came in handy in Mr Charlton's eighth grade World History class. He expected a lot from a bunch of 13-year-olds and, for that, I'm grateful. Between our forays into cartography, we would debate topics like abortion, federal versus states rights and creationism versus evolution. Every time we approached a new topic, I would show up at the Christian book store in search of facts to prepare me for battle. I was a good soldier—well-armed against the attacks of my 13-year-old foes in the desks across the classroom. And often I won (or, at least that's how I remember it).

Those debates, and the reading I did for them, set a particular foundation for me: one of viewing my faith as a set of facts and figures that armed me for war. Being a better Christian meant learning *more* in order to stand up to the non-religious villains at my public school. My church helped by providing courses on cults and the evidence for a young earth and reinforcing my desire to acquire more knowledge so I could be sent into the battlefield of the mind. The mission? To convince people what they believed was wrong and what I believed was right.

I adopted an attitude that every question that *could* be asked had already been asked; and, more importantly, it had been answered by experts who knew a lot more about the subject than I did. Everything about my life and faith was answerable, definable, and package-able. And if it wasn't, chances were it could be answered with some sort of "you gotta have faith" or "God doesn't work that way anymore" mantra. Everything about my faith was set in the past. But as I've discovered since then, and as we'll uncover in this book, this is not the case. God is doing so much. We've just forgotten how to see it. Discovering the depths of God takes exploration.

In the process of believing there must be more, I've softened. I've discovered being willing to ask questions is a lot more important than having all the answers. I have a suspicion you feel the same way and have been waiting for a safe place to be able to ask those questions. That's what I want this journey to be: a safe place to explore.

I realize exploration might rub against the western, Evangelical construct which loves absolute truth. If you're someone who has been shaped and formed by this atmosphere, you might find yourself wanting me to make statements as if I'm absolutely sure about them. That way, when you disagree with something, you can categorize and dismiss—not only the statement—but me, too. But I believe there's a better picture of how we, The Church, can engage with one another—one in which we move from cynicism to hope, one in which we believe we can actually make things better.

A POSTURE OF HOPE

Cynicism and bitterness are poison. If we look at the past with cynicism and bitterness, we're already defeated. We are partially products of the past, and if we live only focused on the flaws of our foundation, we are hopeless.

Most of my life has been lived as a cynic. It's the easiest way to live. When we perceive something as broken, we turn our nose up to it, declare we're better than it and walk away. If this book causes you to walk away thinking you're better than other people or superior to them, it would be better if it were never written at all.

I grew up in a conservative, Evangelical culture, and every time the word "prophet" was used, it was in reference to a bunch of people who lived thousands of years ago. In all my years of growing up, I only heard one person declare himself a prophet—and for him, it was just an excuse to be a jackass. His theological soapbox gave him permission to see things that were broken, to stand at a distance and yell at them. Honestly, I was kind of thankful for him because I wanted to be a jackass too. I loved the thought that I could show up in a place or a relationship or a scenario and spout off all the things I didn't like about it.

Then, one day, I came to the point of new understanding: the prophet and the cynic both have the ability to see. The difference is a cynic sees what's broken about today. A prophet sees what's beautiful about tomorrow.

Just because something is true doesn't mean it's best to say it whenever, wherever, however, and to whomever we want. Wisdom and discernment are gifts of the Spirit. Paul, when talking to the Corinthians, says, "The spirits of prophets are subject to the control of prophets" (1 Corinthians 14:32). He's pointing out the need for a prophet to use restraint and discernment when speaking the things he or she sees. There is a time and a place for everything, and our job is to ask the Holy Spirit, "What?" "When?" "Where?" "Why?" and "How?" I've learned *how* I say what I say is as important as what I say in the first place. I've learned I communicate as much—if not more—through my tone and body language than through my words.

The more I fell in love with Jesus, the more I loved. The more I loved, the more I cared about the Church. The more I cared about the Church, the more I saw it *not* as an organization hell-bent on accomplishing an agenda or executing programs, but as a web of people in relationship with one another. If I do what I do and say what I say and do not love, I should remain silent. But I believe what you and I are called to is far too important to keep silent. So we must love.

IDEAS AND FRIENDS

A few years ago, I read the book *Outliers* by Malcolm Gladwell. In it, he talks about the idea that we become an expert at something only after we've done it for 10,000 hours. At a prestigious music school in the northeast, he asked professors to rate their violin students: which ones would be music teachers, which would play full-time in an orchestra, which would be first chair violinists and which would be solo concert violinists. By measuring the professor's ratings against the number of hours each student had practiced, Gladwell was able (for the most part) to see firsthand the connection between practice hours and skill. The more practice over their lifetime, the more talented the violinist.

This sent me, briefly, into a philosophical spin. What had I done for 10,000 hours? Was my time too divided to be proficient at any one thing? Was I a musician or a writer or a speaker? What was I?! Then it came to me—of the various things I had spent my time doing, these two were consistent: creating community and shifting paradigms.

I hope to achieve both those things through this book. In these pages, I hope you find ideas that resonate with you, and I hope it will spark conversations that result in deep, meaningful relationships. I pray it will create community among people at differing points in their experience (or non-experience) with Jesus. I hope for a great manifestation of unity in the Church, locally and globally, by giving us permission to come together and discuss significant things about our past, present, and future. I pray we will move into an era where we can stand united on the elements of our faith which align, rather than divide over increasingly insignificant disagreements.

I also hope to help shift our paradigms—paradigms about what it means to be human, what it means to be the Church and what it means to be in relationship with God.

The trouble is this: shifting paradigms is relationally difficult. In the past, I loved a good debate. But now, I don't love it. In fact, I often dread it. I'm continually walking the line of unity and prophecy, of peace and stirring the pot. Shifting paradigms can be anxiety-inducing for me. I love people (which has made it difficult to sit by myself even long enough to write this book) and the last thing I want to do is alienate myself from relationships.

I know there will be people who reject the things I say here, and, in the end—ultimately reject me. But I think these things are too important to not be said. Our siloed church culture means we take sides and cut ties with those not in our bubble. I hope to change that. I hope, as you read, together we can find a common place to stand. If you picked up this book, chances are you're someone who wants to explore. To you I say, welcome! I think we can shift things. We can thrust our culture (Christians and otherwise) to a healthier place of life, cooperation, and relationship.

SPIRITUAL INNOVATION

Spiritual Innovation is the idea that, if God is infinite, then surely there is more to be discovered about who God is and how He's working. We'll explore how our narrow criteria of how and where we can experience God keeps us from finding him, and we'll begin to see how, when we open ourselves up to Him, we discover Him in the most unexpected places.

I hope we open ourselves to the possibility that there might be so much more for us than we ever imagined. At the very least, I hope you discover a new freedom for yourself—the freedom to dream again and dream bigger. But ultimately, I hope for something so much more—that your dreaming will manifest itself as noticeable, tangible shifts in the world around you.

This is the cultural shift I'm talking about. Do you know you have the power to change your surrounding atmosphere?

So often we discount our ability to walk into a room and shift the atmosphere. We understand the power of music to do this. That's why there's background music playing almost everywhere we go. We understand that the way something sounds or smells or feels (like temperature) can change the entire attitude of a room. But we forget *we* have this same power. Something as simple as a smile can shift the reality around you, and even more so the power of the Holy Spirit revealed through you. This is the concept of Spiritual Innovation—that you have the ability to access the unseen, to participate in the work of God, and to radically shift the world by living with supernatural wisdom.

There are people who will read that statement and think, "Hm. Right now, I'm questioning whether or not God even exists, let alone if He's working and wants me to participate in it." Maybe you're one of those people. Well, I think you're in exactly the right place to be encountering this book. I have so many friends who have given up on God and I don't blame them. We've been fed a powerless, impotent religion in the form of American Evangelicalism. But it's time to take back the power our faith has always had from the beginning. It's time to see a new reformation that demonstrates the power of God in ways we've never encountered before. It's time to allow his love and grace to drip from us and into the world around us.

It's a new way of thinking about your faith.
This is Spiritual Innovation.

SPIRITUAL INNOVATION

I pray this book will help launch us into a different cultural reality—one of asking questions and expecting more. One in which we, filled with the mind of Christ and the Holy Spirit, contribute to society, rather than continually tearing it to pieces. One in which we no longer anticipate and hope for cultural destruction but lead the way in helping our earth resemble heaven.

"I might be completely wrong, but..." I think this is what God wants.

SPIRITUAL INNOVATION // CHAPTER ONE
SOMETHING IS MISSING

SPIRITUAL INNOVATION

Have you ever felt like your life with God was powerless; like there is supposed to be more? Have you ever wondered why there seems to be such a gap between the lives of the people you see in the Bible and your life today?

It was a rainy, late summer evening and I had walked a few blocks through the Florida night to a bar down the street from my house to meet some friends. When I got there, the friends I had come to meet hadn't yet arrived but another friend, Nick, was sitting by the pool table with some guys. I walked over to say hi.

Nick and I had known each other for a long time. In fact, we led worship together in the first year of our friendship. By the time I ran into him at the bar, we were still friends, but found ourselves in different places of belief.

Somehow, the conversation shifted quickly from small talk. Nick looked over at me and said, "You know, the things you believe as a Christian can be reached by many other means—other religions, other philosophies."

"Yep." I acknowledged. He was right. There are a lot of wonderful people who believe all kinds of things apart from Christianity—who are doing amazing things to make the world a better place. Then I went on.

"But I don't believe that's the way it's supposed to be. The Church has lost something over the last 1500 years or so. Following Christ used to include a powerful demonstration of something otherworldly—for the sake of God's glory and the revelation of the kingdom of heaven on earth. Today, that's what's missing."

I frequently have conversations with people who are disillusioned with their experience with the American Evangelical Church, conversations like the one I had with Nick. I share many of the things you'll read in the coming chapters of this book, and the people I share these things with often respond in a similar way as Nick: "Yeah, but what you're talking about isn't Christianity. It's something else."

In some ways that comment is true. Many people who are practicing the Christian faith today are living a sterilized version of what it means to follow Jesus. Honestly, most of the time, that's my reality too. The picture I paint in this book is a life of immense power, liberated from the systems we've created to make us feel safe and to control other people. But do I live that kind of life? Not always.

So, Nick was right. The life I'm talking about seems far removed from our modern Evangelical Christian experience; but in that, I believe it becomes all the more Christian.

The longer I talked with Nick, the more I started to uncover an idea I think is really important: People (myself included) don't need the Jesus of Evangelical Christianity—at least not the way he's been presented. Think about it: he's an impotent character of good ideologies. He has been stripped of power, sealed in a completely "knowable" package, and delivered to us as a product we can control. It seems we've taken a faith meant to be wild, confusing, mysterious, tangible, active, and powerful and reduced it to something manageable and comfortable.

But when I read the Bible and encounter stories about the sea parting and bushes burning and paralyzed men being healed with a touch—I have to ask myself: doesn't it seem like we're missing something?

THERE'S SOMETHING ABOUT MYSTERY

From a young age, I was drawn to the mysterious. I haven't seen Unsolved Mysteries in over a decade, but if you ask me the phone number, it's immediately accessible in my head: 1-800-876-5353. Every

SPIRITUAL INNOVATION

Wednesday night, after attending Awana Club at a medium-sized Southern Baptist Church in Orlando, my family and I would head to my grandparents' house, and while the adults talked, I would try to watch Unsolved Mysteries. I still get chills on the back of my neck at the thought of Robert Stack's voice and that synthesized theme song. Even as I write this, I want to move my feet up onto the couch to make sure they're out of reach from whatever's hiding under there.

The "Lost Loves" segments were bearable at best. These were the segments where people were trying to find loved ones from their past. The "Unexplained/Alternative History" segments were alright. But it was the "Paranormal Matters" I was really after. Something in those stories about Bigfoot, the Loch Ness Monster, Miracles, UFOs and ghosts really captured my attention. It was the beginning of a love for the mysterious—or maybe even the initial revelation of a desire God had planted inside me early on. I hadn't quite discovered the right way to cultivate it, but during Unsolved Mysteries, I remember it being there.

After Unsolved Mysteries, it was the X-Files, reruns of The Twilight Zone, and a movie about a famous alien abduction called "Fire In The Sky". I remember going to Washington D.C. with my mom, aunt, and brother one summer and buying a "Haunted D.C." book that I had read several times through by the time we got home to Florida. And every time we'd head to St Augustine, FL, I made sure a trip to the original *Ripley's Believe It Or Not* was in the plans.

Of course, I was completely terrified at the thought of actually *encountering* a ghost or an alien or anything remotely part of the supernatural world. It was a common occurrence for me to take the trash out at night, and if I ever did this after watching a scary movie, I would run from the front door in my boxer shorts, throw the trash bag into the can as quickly as possible, sprint back to the front door—out of breath—and lock it behind me, all the while chanting the name of Jesus.

It was apparent from a young age, that I was drawn to the mysterious. I was a childhood mystic. I loved the thought of the unknown. To this day, I relish the reality of things beyond what I can see.

To contrast my love for the mysterious, I grew up in Baptist-dom. For all the flack Baptists tend to get, it's actually something I'm really thankful I was able to experience. But when I was beginning middle school, my family transitioned to a wonderfully un-Baptist Baptist church and that gave me a good foundation in scripture and just enough freedom to explore charisma and keep me engaged. In the traditional Baptist way, there was little mention of the Holy Spirit and certainly no expectation for the supernatural.

So I've spent the last 13 years of my adult life discovering, from scratch, the possibility that things are meant to be a little different than the safe, rigid, systematic church experience I had for the first 18 years of my life.

I grew up in (and am thankful to still be in) Orlando, FL. For many people, it's the place where dreams come true—at least in childhood. Orlando is the land of Disney. It's the first US city to have reached 60 million visitors in a calendar year. And many of those visitors are families coming to have an experience with one another they can't find anywhere else. Walt Disney World is built on the idea that we can immerse ourselves in the fantastic stories of our childhoods. We can fly with Peter Pan. We can swim through the ocean with Ariel. We can travel through a real life Haunted Mansion and we can actually shake hands and take a picture with a 5 foot 5 inch bipedal mouse.

I first worked for the Walt Disney Company when I was in the fourth grade. What an awesome thing to walk into my fourth grade classroom and tell them, "I'm coming to class late because I was at a rehearsal at Disney World until 1am this morning. It was so cool. Between rehearsals, I was allowed to walk around with my mom.

SPIRITUAL INNOVATION

There was *no one* else even in the park. Did I mention it was cool?" Being there and seeing behind-the-scenes only served to draw me into the magic even more. There was something very real about the magic happening there.

Then, more than 10 years later, Universal Orlando opened the Wizarding World of Harry Potter. About a year before that section of the park was scheduled to open, I got a call from a company here in town. "Hey, we're working on a show for Harry Potter. We'd love if you could help us workshop the show." I told them to give me a day to think about it and I'd let them know.

To "workshop" a show meant the writers, directors, producers, techs, and performers would all come together in a room and bring the show to life for the first time. It sounded like something that would be really fun, but 1) I knew nothing about Harry Potter and 2) all these Christians were saying bad things about it being satanic and such.

I decided to do it.

After immersing myself in the Wizarding World of Harry Potter for a couple of weeks, I began to think about why this would be so threatening to Christians. Why were they up in arms about this stuff? It all seemed innocent enough. And then it hit me: regardless of why fundamentalists *said* they were afraid of Harry Potter, the reason they *should* be afraid is because he's way more powerful than they are.

From my time spent with the team at the Wizardly World of Harry Potter, I would say he seems pretty awesome. He says these sets of magic words and waves a wand about and wham, stuff happens.

We Christians, though, we say what we think are magic words, we hope really hard, we squeeze our eyes tightly shut, we open them and—most often—things are exactly the same as they were before.

If Harry challenged us to a dual, most of the time we'd lose. But looking at the Bible, that doesn't really seem to add up. Dumbledore dies at the end of the series and yet, When Jesus' friends die in the Bible, he raises them from the dead. So maybe Christians are just afraid of Harry because he reminds us of who we are supposed to be.

The Harry Potter series has sold over 450 million copies and millions of people have taken a pilgrimage to Universal Orlando to get the closest they can to a real life Hogwarts experience. To me, this is the outliving of Romans 8:19, or at least a reflection of it: "The creation waits in eager expectation for the sons of God to be revealed."

When I was a child, I knew there was something more. I knew there was something I could not see that was waiting to be discovered—something with the ability to awaken the physical realm to a deeper spiritual reality. The rest of humanity—in fact, all of creation—knows the same thing. The only problem (and it's a big problem) is the very ones who have been entrusted with the opportunity to bring this supernatural power into existence have forgotten they hold the keys to this great gift.

We don't need to be afraid of Harry Potter. We hold something more powerful than fantasy.

ON THE WAY UP

One Sunday night, my friend Trent was speaking at our church. He had recently read Andy Crouch's "Culture Making" and was inspired by the charge for the church to become Creative Cultivators of the cosmos. Trent is the kind of guy who—even in a room of 600—will have conversations with people from the stage. He'd often ask questions and wait for people to answer. After a couple years of teaching, he had our congregation conditioned to his question-asking. So this time the answers came quickly.

"If the fall had never happened," he began, "what would earth be like today?"

"Pandora," one guy said, and everyone pretty much agreed. The hundreds of people gathered in that room—many of them professional creatives—were at a loss for any other answer. Pandora is the planet inhabited by the Na'vi in the movie Avatar, a land in which its inhabitants lived in harmony with the natural world.

James Cameron's imaginings of what the world could or should be like—Pandora, until the humans showed up—did seem to be a fairly accurate picture of what we see painted of the kingdom of God in scripture. It was a land of peace. There was peace among the living beings and peace in their relationship with their environment. It was a land of beauty. And while there was death, the Na'vi lived on in relationship with their ancestors. It was a picture right out of the pages of Isaiah where the lion lays down with the lamb—there is no more sickness and an overwhelming peace persists throughout the natural world.

But is that possible, this side of heaven?

Are we, the Church, willing to pray the same prayer Jesus prayed: "Thy kingdom come. Thy will be done..."?

For most of us, the utopia of the kingdom of heaven is a distant reality—if even a reality at all. We think it's something unattainable, out of reach, for someone other than us in a time different than ours. But what does it mean that Jesus taught us to pray, "Thy kingdom come. Thy will be done, on earth as it is in heaven."? Jesus wasn't talking about a future reality. He was saying, "the time of the coming of the kingdom of heaven is now." Jesus' example is present tense.

In Luke 4, Jesus goes to the temple. Usually the people in the temple read the scriptures from a scroll sequentially—one passage after the next, from day to day. In Luke 4, Jesus "found the place where it is written..." Jesus wasn't haphazardly opening the scroll or turning to a random place. He picked up the scroll and intentionally found the words spoken by the prophet Isaiah:

"The Spirit of the Lord is on me, because he has anointed me to preach good news to the poor. He has sent me to proclaim freedom for the prisoners and recovery of sight for the blind, to release the oppressed, to proclaim the year of the Lord's favor."

Then Jesus, after reading these words, said, "Today this scripture is fulfilled in your hearing." He didn't say "some day in the future, these words will be fulfilled." He didn't say, "in another time and place this will happen." He said, "Today this scripture is fulfilled in your hearing." So what does that mean for us?

It means that for the last 2,000 years, the Church has had the opportunity to live in the complete fullness of Jesus' proclamation that He has completed the work of bringing good news to the poor. It means every prisoner has the opportunity to be completely free. It means Jesus has released power for every blind person to have sight, and we are living in the year of the Lord's favor. That work has been completed.

But our experience often doesn't align with the words and commissioning of Jesus. So what do we do? We create nice, pseudo-scriptural phrases like "already, but not yet" to convey the idea that Jesus completed the work of salvation on the cross but we live in a broken, fallen, degrading world. From a scriptural standpoint, I'd suggest the phrase, "already and increasing" is the more helpful and honest posture for us to take.

Let me paint you a picture.

We have Moses. He has fled to the desert to escape possible prosecution for the murder of an Egyptian guard. There, he spends many years of his life as a shepherd. One day, he notices a bush. It's on fire. "Surely it'll burn out soon," he thinks. Yet the bush just keeps burning. Then he notices the bush, while it's on fire, is not being consumed by the fire at all. Eventually, out the of the bush comes a voice—the voice of God—who commissions Moses to lead the people of Israel out of captivity and into the promised land. Accompanying this process is miracle after miracle. I don't think we'd argue Moses lived a pretty miraculous life.

Then comes Elijah. He summons 450 prophets of Baal and 400 prophets of Asherah to Mount Carmel where two altars are built—one for Baal and one for Yahweh. He says to the prophets, "Alright, go ahead and pray that fire will fall down and consume the altar." They get to praying, without success. They begin to mutilate their bodies thinking, perhaps a blood sacrifice will do the trick. (I suppose they were right... just the wrong blood). Night comes, and no fire has arrived.

Can you just imagine their conversation?

"Alright now, here's Yahweh's altar. I want to show you just how amazing God is, so let's do this right. You guys go get 3 large jars of water and pour it all over the wood on the altar." They do as Elijah asks. "No. You know what? That's not enough. How about doing that two more times. I really want to make sure the wood is good and soaked." Again, they do it. "Alright God, you do what you do," Elijah prays. Immediately fire falls from the sky, consuming the offering, the wood, and the altar itself. Then Elijah prays for a release of rain from the sky, which God does, ending a three-and-a-half year famine.

Then comes Joshua, who leads the people of Israel across the Jordan river on dry ground; Jonah, whom God sends with a message to the people of Nineveh; Daniel, who interprets dreams, survives a fiery furnace, and finds favor in the eyes of the king; Samuel, who hears God's voice audibly calling him into ministry; and all the other Old Testament prophets who deliver God's words to the world.

Finally, along comes John the Baptist. Before his birth, the priest, John's father Zechariah, is given a word from an angel about who John is and his divine role. John has been sent to prepare the way for the coming Messiah.

John sets Jesus up to enter into his public ministry, and, in Matthew 11, Jesus says of John, "I tell you the truth: Among those born of women there has not risen anyone greater than John the Baptist..." That means John is greater, in the scope of the kingdom, than all the patriarchs and prophets who have performed incomprehensible miracles and demonstrated awesome works of God's power before him—Moses, Elijah, Joshua, Jonah... all of them.

Is it possible we have access to this same power, and more?

FROM THE ANCIENT TO THE MODERN

In 2014, Darren Aronofsky released his film, Noah. There was an uproar from much of the Evangelical community asking, "is it Biblically accurate?" What they were really asking was, "did Aronofsky get all the facts correct?" and "did he add anything else to the story that's not specifically recorded in the Bible?"

But I wonder if those are the right questions to ask about an artistic re-telling of a biblical story. If you read the story of Noah in Genesis, what you'll quickly discover is that it feels much more like the reporting of details than it does the telling of a story. In fact, much of the Bible is expository (analytical telling of facts), and even when a story is being conveyed, it feels far more like a series of events laid out in a news article than an engaging narrative.

I think that sometimes leads us to unnecessarily separate ourselves from the people in the Bible—to act as if they were somehow different than we are. This is the beauty of storytellers like Aronofsky. He can read between the lines and ask, "what makes this person human? What might they have felt in this moment? What were his fears and joys and pains?" As he brings these things to life, you and I can realize Noah and the other Biblical characters were just as real as you and me.

The power we see demonstrated in the life of Moses or Elijah or Jonah or John the Baptist is just the beginning. We are the continuation of the story.

Jesus affirms John as greater than the prophets who have come before him, but continues on: "yet he who is least in the kingdom of heaven is greater than he." In this passage, Jesus is talking about you and me—those who are found in Christ, from that moment forward. We are those who belong to the kingdom of heaven. And this declaration is only the beginning of what Jesus says about what we are to accomplish through him.

I tell you the truth, anyone who has faith in me will do what I have been doing. He will do even greater things than these, because I am going to the Father. (John 14:12)

Jesus tells us we will accomplish not only the miraculous works he accomplished while here on the earth, but *even greater* things. Cessationists would have us believe Jesus is referring to the work of presenting the good news for the salvation of humanity, and while that is a wonderful work, I would argue Jesus is making a clear declaration in this passage of the miracles his followers will accomplish here on earth. Jesus gives us a mysterious and prophetic declaration of "greater things than these."

Jesus' declaration of power was not only a word for those who stood within hearing distance that day. It wasn't a promise meant only for those who had seen Jesus face-to-face as a confirmation of their message. Mark specifically records Jesus using the phrase "whoever believes" and in the next verse says, "and these signs will accompany those who believe..." Here, Jesus is making a broad statement about the new reality that came to fruition as the result of his work on the cross and his conquering of death in resurrection.

This upward slope of increased power continues throughout the New Testament. It is prophesied by Peter when he stands up at Pentecost and recites a prophesy from Joel. The society of Peter's day was similar to our modern Church in this way: it restricted who God would use to accomplish His work. There were only certain people worthy of demonstrating the gifts of His Spirit. But Peter stands up on this day, full of the Holy Spirit, and affirms the work of the Spirit through old as well as young, men as well as women. The same is true for us today. The power of the Spirit is now to be manifested through all people. (Acts 2:17-18)

This discussion of the increasing breadth of the indwelling of the Holy Spirit continues into Paul's letters to the churches. He tells the people of Galatia:

There is neither Jew nor Greek, slave nor free, male nor female, for you are all one in Christ Jesus. If you belong to Christ, then you are Abraham's seed, and heirs according to the promise.

And the work of God, not just salvation but the power of the Holy Spirit to heal, help, and revive is meant to continue right into today—directly into your life and mine.

A WHOLE NEW WORLD

As God was busy increasing the scope of those through whom He would make Himself known, He was also reminding us of his original intention for redemption. We so often think of salvation in the terms of the the eternal resting place of the spirit of a person, but from the very beginning, we see God's heart for salvation is much broader than that.

The whole of the Old Testament is the story of the "chosen people," but from the very beginning, God makes His intent very clear: it is to bless Abraham so "all peoples on earth will be blessed through you."

In the New Testament, we see that plan for continual increase of God's favor and kingdom revealed over the entire earth. Paul becomes more liberal in his declaration of God's redemption. No longer is it solely for a group of chosen people designed to declare God's redemption. It's not only for human beings. God's heart for redemption is for *all* of creation. God is reconciling *all* things to himself.

For God was pleased to have all his fullness dwell in him [Jesus], and through him to reconcile to himself all things, whether things on earth or things in heaven, by making peace through his blood, shed on the cross. (Colossians 1:19-20)

And he has chosen to have us co-labor with him in the process of reconciling all of creation back to himself. The writer of Romans says, "creation waits in eager expectation for the sons of God to be revealed" so that it will be "liberated from its bondage to decay and brought into the glorious freedom of the children of God." (Romans 8:19-21)

In other words, the salvation of Jesus isn't simply so we can go to heaven or sit around in a spiritual stupor. There are very tangible effects of redemption. We are rescued for a purpose. And, while so many use the Genesis command to "subdue the earth and rule over it" as an excuse for raping and abusing it, I believe God wants to reveal His original intention for the earth through His people. We are empowered to establish the peace of God on the earth.

So we see this process of increase over the whole of scripture—from the Old Testament to John the Baptist to Jesus to those of us in the kingdom. We see a continual increase in the scope of God's revelation of his power and his kingdom, to and through all people in Christ, even unto creation. But there's still more.

In Ephesians, Paul writes that we not only reveal the fullness of Christ to the physical, earthly realm but also to the spiritual realm. He writes, "that now, through the church, the manifold wisdom of God should be made known to the rulers and authorities in the heavenly realms, according to his eternal purpose which he accomplished in Christ Jesus our Lord." (Ephesians 3:10-11) Can you imagine that we would be ordained to reveal God's glory, even to the heavenly realm? What an incredible task. What an amazing honor.

The reality is this: there are things God is revealing through you and me, His Church, that heretofore have yet to be revealed, even in the spiritual realm. That this manifold, multifaceted wisdom is continuing to be unveiled should not surprise us, as we're talking about an unlimited, unending, ultimate, all-encompassing creator God who has no limit. It's to be expected that His glory, which is ever-increasing, would never finish it's growing expression of God through us here on the earth.

And we, who with unveiled faces all reflect the Lord's glory, are being transformed into his likeness with ever-increasing glory, which comes from the Lord, who is the Spirit. (2 Cor 3:18)

Moses covered his face in shame because he didn't want people to see God's radiating glory (what he had gained as a result of his time with God) fading. But Paul declares, on the backside of the cross, that God's glory—and subsequently His kingdom—are not fading, but rather increasing in us, on us, and through us unto the earth.

SPIRITUAL INNOVATION

Harry Potter and Avatar are good stories of a fantastic existence but they are not the real story. They remind us of the deep, spiritual power we're meant to live out. But as sons and daughters of God, we don't need magic spells or wands or castles. We have resurrection power inside us. We have a perfect kingdom at our fingertips. And we are sons and daughters of the Creator and orchestrator of everything.

It's time we reawaken to the stories of our past as recorded in the pages of the Bible. It's time we treat those accounts not as fantasy, but as the first chapter in a story that has, for the most part, laid dormant for 1500 years.

You see, those stories in the book of Acts were just the beginning of a mighty move of God set into motion to fulfill how Jesus taught us to pray: "Thy kingdom come. Thy will be done on earth as it is in heaven." We've been born into a world that has long forgotten what the kingdom looks like. But Jesus taught us to pray for the kingdom of heaven—in all it's perfection and beauty—in the present tense. Our attempts to regain the kingdom—the best human ingenuity, creativity and intellect we can muster—are only the beginning if we trust in the promise that we are able to do things even greater than the things Jesus did while he was here on earth.

That's Spiritual Innovation. And it's a crazy idea. The reality God's been revealing Himself to and through humanity for millennia—it's hard to wrap our brains around. And even more that that, He's not done!

The world is doing a darn good job at bringing its longing for the kingdom to fruition through science and technology. And even when it's nothing more than the stories of fantasy and science fiction they're still dreaming of what's yet to be uncovered.

So what happened to us—the Church—along the way?

QUESTIONS AND CONVERSATIONS :

Spiritual Innovation isn't just about the way we think. It's about the way we live. These questions–at the end of each chapter–are designed to help you take the ideas you've read about and begin moving forward in your daily life. Take time to consider these. Write your answers out. Or, better yet, have a conversation with some friends.

- What are the biggest differences between the life you live and the things you see in the lives of the people in the Bible? Why do you think those differences exist? Should they?

- Do you run from or embrace the mystery of your faith? Why?

- Are there things to still be discovered? How can you set yourself up to encounter the unexpected in your everyday life?

DO SOMETHING :

This section–at the end of each chapter–is designed to give you something practical to do to get outside yourself and expect Spiritual Innovation in your life.

There are several examples in this chapter of people in the Bible (and in fiction) who have put themselves in situations that are bigger than they are–situations beyond their ability and control. Put yourself in a moment that is bigger than your ability. Look for how God wants to reveal the realities of heaven in that moment, and discover how you can be a conduit through which God delivers heaven.

SPIRITUAL INNOVATION // CHAPTER TWO
HOW DID WE GET HERE
OUR INDIVIDUAL NEED FOR CONTROL

SPIRITUAL INNOVATION

It was a Wednesday night. I was 17 years old. Our youth pastor had just left our church to go to another one and we had a fantastic youth worker sitting in as the interim youth leader.

"My grandmother really believes Jesus will return before she dies," he said "and I'm inclined to believe it. When you look at the signs of the times, when you look at what's going on in our world, it just makes sense." He was about 40 when he said that. I assume his grandmother was at least 70. That was 15 years ago. So statistically, she's no longer alive, and Jesus hasn't come back yet.

In every generation since Jesus ascended, there have been people who swear they will be the last generation before he returns again. Even Peter did it. After Jesus ascended, he went back to fishing and he and the disciples just waited for Jesus to return. Eventually, Jesus showed back up and told them to get a move on—to stop wasting time, to get up and spread the kingdom. He commissioned them.

They did some amazing things for awhile, but for the most part, they forgot about those amazing things and went back to their fishing. Look around. Wouldn't you say we have done the same? We have forgotten about the amazing things that are possible and have gone back to our metaphorical fishing. Western evangelicals have, for the most part, thrown their hands up in the air and said, "The world is going to hell in a hand basket. Things are too far gone for me to do anything about it, so let's just get ready and wait for Jesus to hurry up and get back here." In the meantime, we've gotten good at managing things the way they are without much thought to the prayer Jesus taught so long ago: "Thy kingdom come. Thy will be done, on earth as it is in heaven."

CONTROLLERS

We love control. Let's go all the way back to the first pages of the

Bible—to the Garden of Eden. There's Adam and Eve and God and a serpent. There's the Tree of Life and the Tree of the Knowledge of Good and Evil.

The Tree of Life represented dependency on God for everything we, as humans, needed physically and spiritually. The Tree of the Knowledge of Good and Evil represented our desire to come up with our own solutions for life. It was to say, "I don't need you, God. I can do this on my own." Chances are, this is a feeling you're familiar with. There are lots of examples throughout the rest of the Bible, in my life and maybe in your life too.

We often think about approaching God in the "big" decisions and relying on our own ability to control everything else. In Numbers 20, the Israelites are thirsty, as they've been wandering around the desert. God tells Moses to speak to a rock and water will flow from it. But Moses decides to strike the rock with his staff instead. God chastises Moses for not trusting in Him and—as a result—not honoring him.

In your life, maybe you're willing to pray about a big decision—a relationship, where to live, where to go to school, a new job. But in what you consider to be the small decisions, you try to make it on your own. Every time we relinquish control (in both the large and small decisions), we trust God and honor Him.

Control feels good. It gives us a sense of security, the sense we can prevent anything unexpected from happening. So we create systems and rules to get things to look just like we want them to look. Usually this leaves us with the appearance of control on the surface, but a deep level of turmoil and anxiety underneath. When our security is built on control, our lives are given over to maintaining and protecting that control, which is a totally exhausting, full-time job.

This is the job of an addict, who must control the way he or she feels with the use of alcohol or drugs. This is the job of an anorexic, who must control the way he or she looks by limiting food intake to a bare minimum. And this is the job of the overly "religious" person, who follows the letter of the law but has never experienced the freedom of Grace.

The need for control is not new for us—it manifests itself throughout the Bible as well. In the Old Testament, we come to the people of Israel who have been delivered from Egypt. They have established themselves in the promised land and they now want a king—someone they can touch and see and listen to and, when necessary, blame. Although God has clearly rescued them from their terrible circumstances, they want someone they can encounter with their senses on a daily basis. God says, basically, "It's not the best idea, but okay." Along comes Saul as their king.

But the desire for control in the lives of these Biblical characters didn't get them what they ultimately wanted. It led to more distance between them and God. This progression seems natural to me: when we have the illusion of control, we think we no longer need God. We venture out into life detached from the source of life. Not only does control lead us to a place anxiety, exhaustion, and a nearly neurotic need to maintain it, but control disconnects us from divine relationship.

Yet the pattern continues throughout recorded history. Our desire for control over land and resources, people and wealth, and our own lives has led us into wars and arguments and systems and plans in every human context—individually, as families, villages, cities, states, and nations.

Part of this desire for control is inborn and part of it is culturally instilled. Let's take a very simple summary of the Industrial Revolution as our example.

Up until the Industrial Revolution, a majority of the American population lived in rural areas. Many of them were farmers and most were uneducated. The boom of the Industrial Revolution led people, in increasing numbers, to major cities looking for work and the work was there. The problem was that the education was *not*. These farmers didn't know how to operate machinery or, often, read instruction manuals. So a system was put in place to accommodate for the problem.

We would put an educational system in place to teach as many people the same information as quickly as possible for the sake of supporting the industrial infrastructure. The goal was to have a controllable and manageable system; and the result was a system that saw people as robots (eventually even replaced them with robots). Each student became replaceable. Hence, our modern educational system was born and persists, in large part, to this day.

As a reflection of this time, much of our educational infrastructure still operates as if all students learn the same way, need to learn the same thing, have the same ability and are all cut out for the same work. We know this is not the case, but this mindset of sameness was born out of control during the Industrial Revolution and has permeated our culture more broadly since then.

In the church, we create programs that will process as many people as possible by feeding them the same spiritual information in a system that is efficient and clean.

I'm a part of leading a church called City Beautiful Church in Orlando, and one of the things we've said often at our church is "Ain't no formula." Of course, we live in a world of order and rhythm. So creating systems and strategies can be healthy and helpful. But the difference between order and rhythm and *formula* is found deep in our hearts.

Bringing order from chaos is such a beautiful thing that we, as God's image-bearers, have the ability to do. We certainly see order and rhythm in the world around us and there are great things we learn from these realities. Spiritual and physical rhythms are important. But again, order and rhythm are different from formulas.

Order and rhythm differentiate from formulas in this way. Formulas lead us to say, "every time I encounter X situation, I respond with Y. Rather than being present in the moment, listening spiritually and responding in obedience, I have figured out the right answer for every person, in every circumstance, everywhere. I will not only hold myself to this standard of Y but others as well."

Often, our formulas lead us to lean on our own understanding, rather than acknowledge God in all our ways.

We want to live by formulas, because we think it'll make life easier. But a life lived by formulas is not really living at all.

I grew up in a church culture of formulas—what to do, what not to do, when and where to do or not do those things. Everything was neatly packaged into formulas and categories. Categories are like comfort food. They're not necessary, but they help us feel good. They tell us who's supposed to do what—like the category of "firefighters." Or they tell us when we can take a break—like with "weekends" or "holidays."

But I think one of the reasons we like categories so much is because they allow us to feel like we're in control. When we meet someone, categories allow us to immediately make a decision about who we think this person is. And, as a result, we can almost immediately assess whether, in our own minds, they are valuable to us. You see, I think categories, like comfort foods, are mostly bad for us.

Look at the idea of nationalities. When two countries engage in a war, one of the first forms of propaganda is to make the "enemy" a nameless, faceless hyperbole. We see images of turban-headed, bomb-toting caricatures of "Iraqis" rather than the faces of individuals—with stories, families, hurts, and happiness.

Categorization allows us to write people off. Like the phrase, "Oh, they're just Charismatic Christians." In long form, someone who would say this most likely means, "Oh, that person—with their flailing arms and barefoot dancing—most likely isn't genuine in his or her spiritual experience. He or she is just copying what they've seen other people in that Charismatic Christian category do." It allows us to write off the individual and frees us from asking if their experience means something for us.

You can replace "Charismatic Christian" with pretty much any category: "the gays," "the Jews," "boys," "girls," "men," "women" and you'll get the same result. Disconnection—both from the people themselves and from our thoughts and feelings about them.

After the categorization and formation of opinion when it comes to people in a certain category, we begin creating systems for how we will respond to anyone we encounter from that category. We'll convert non-Christians, be wary of the gays, never answer to door to Mormons and refuse to make eye-contact with anyone wearing a turban. These systems allow us to ignore relationship and maintain our stereotypes.

In Jesus' day, there were lots of people claiming to be the Messiah. So when Jesus came along claiming to be Messiah, most of the pious people—the ones who should have recognized him the most—simply wrote him off as just another guy in the "claiming to be Messiah" category. Their problem was they were trying to stay in control. Meanwhile, he actually *was* who he was claiming to be.

"Tithing" is another example of how Christians sometimes try to maintain control through formulas. And actually, the first time I introduced the phrase, "Ain't no formula" to our church was in a message about giving.

As a kid, I did chores—cleaned the toilet, mowed the yard, dusted my bedroom. The payment for chores was allowance. Each time I did a chore, I ran up to my parent's bedroom, opened the bedside table and pulled out a white pad of paper with a long running ledger of plus and minuses, earnings and payouts. Most Sundays, I would run up to that ledger, pull it out, move the decimal point one place to the left and determine the 10% tithe I was to put in the pink envelope with my church's logo printed on it.

So, 15 years later in life, as I was preparing to give a message about "generosity" at my church, naturally I started researching *the tithe*. The tithe was mentioned in the books of Leviticus, Numbers and Deuteronomy. It was an agricultural offering of one tenth of one's grain, wine, and oil harvests. But continuing on in my preparation, it became obvious: tithe was only one example of sacrificial giving in the Bible.

In Luke 19, Zacceaus, as a result of his encounter with Jesus, gave away half of his possessions and returned four times the amount he had stolen from individuals. When Jesus encounters the Rich Young Ruler in Matthew 19, Jesus instructs him to give away *everything* he has and come follow him. In Acts, we see members of the Church giving away all they had and giving to others as they had need. Even Ananias and Sapphira—after selling their field—were told the money they had received was at their disposal.

So why the ten percent? I think it's because we like control and formulas give us the illusion of control. Encouraging people into a place of freedom takes control away. As individuals, we feel at ease when we know the expectation and can, without thought, meet that expectation. We ask, "what will make God happy with me?" and work to meet the minimum requirement so we can feel at ease. Then, as leaders, if we reinforce ten percent, that gives us a common, consistent message and a sense of peace that we will receive at least that much. But no one needs to be in relationship with God to understand this ten percent rule. The tither need not listen to God for instruction on giving, and the leader need not listen for how to lead his or her people or trust in God for provision.

This control issue just gets more and more complicated the deeper we dig. In our modern context of individualism, rights, and freedoms, we often have the illusion of independence, but we so often have an internal longing to be told what to do. Again, because formulas make us comfortable, we love to find "spiritual leaders" or "pastors" who will go away and study and then come back with formulas for us. Simultaneously, leaders love control. It's addicting, and once we get a taste of it, we often crave it. People want someone to tell them how to live and leaders crave the opportunity to tell them. It's a modern day Tree of Knowledge of Good and Evil. "I don't need to exist in relationship with God because someone else will. They tell me what He says and I do it."

After setting up systems for ourselves, we get to work setting up systems for those around us. "This is how you live." "Here is where you go." "This is what you do." Just like that, we become like little spiritual robots.

SPIRITUAL MACHINES

When Jesus was around, he lived in a culture of stories, questions, parables, and a recognition of something more than the cerebral. Often we see people coming to Jesus to ask questions and yet he doesn't answer them. Rather, he tells them a story and those stories leave people with more questions than answers. To me, there's something really beautiful about this. Jesus' stories don't satisfy every intellectual curiosity. They don't provide black and white answers. Instead they leave people coming back to Jesus again and again, longing for more.

After telling the parable of the sower,

The disciples came to [Jesus] and asked, "Why do you speak to the people in parables?"

He replied, "Because the knowledge of the secrets of the kingdom of heaven has been given to you, but not to them. Whoever has will be given more, and they will have an abundance. Whoever does not have, even what they have will be taken from them. This is why I speak to them in parables:

"Though seeing, they do not see; though hearing, they do not hear or understand. (Matthew 13:10-13)

Jesus knew the hearts of the disciples were postured in such a way that they could derive spiritual truth from the parables he told. In contrast, Jesus went on to explain that those who didn't understand failed to do so because of the callousness of their hearts. In other words, they came to Jesus not to discover the depths of a relationship with God, but to be validated in their own understanding.

We're quick to assume we're on the side of the disciples, but ask yourself honestly: Do you want a relationship with God, or do you want to be right?

Those seeking to satisfy their own understanding will dismiss Jesus' words as frivolous, while those who hang on his words, who wrestle with them, will be able to discover the deeper realities in them. When we believe the best about something—when we look for the divine in it—we discover God there. On the other hand, when we approach it with disdain or preconceived expectation, we miss the unexpected possibilities of discovery.

This is the entire story of Jesus. The religious, with their deep understanding of Old Testament scripture, expected a militant Jesus who would come to forcefully deliver the Jews from the hands of the Romans. The problem was, when the Messiah showed up, they missed him because he didn't meet their expectations.

On the other hand, the New Testament church—the early followers of Christ, filled with the Holy Spirit—knew life was about discovering the unknown depths of God. The book of Acts records some of the fruit that came from their posture of discovery. Thousands came to know Christ, people were healed, and the power of the Holy Spirit was tangibly present in and through the lives of the people. But religiosity is the enemy of a relationship with God. Religion attempts to recreate meaningful spiritual experiences through the analysis and systemization of circumstances. God wants to do something new in each person everyday.

If you've ever been to an improv show, you've probably seen a bad improv scene. You know, the ones where people get on stage and just kind of stare at each other awkwardly. Then someone says, " Uhhhh... hey... what's up?" The other guy says something like, "Oh... not much. Just... uhh... hanging out." Then guy number one replies, "Cool." And they stare at each other some more until, somehow, the scene is put out of its misery.

Well, some well-meaning individuals along the way created some "rules of improv" that are in place to help prevent such a situation. The rules are as follows:

    1. Don't deny.

    2. Don't ask questions.

3. Don't dictate action.

4. Don't talk about past or future events.

5. Say "yes" then say "and."

The list goes on.

In his book, "Improvise," Mick Napier tells the story of how this whole thing came about. At some point he says, there was the first improv scene. Some people were in front of some other people. They started acting out a scene. The people watching began to laugh. It was electric. They kept going! The audience laughed more. The scene ended. They walked off stage, looked at each other and said, "Wow! That was awesome! What just happened, and how can we do it again?"

Soon, other people tried to recreate the experience but something just wasn't happening right. The scenes were getting awkward. They would just stand there and talk about stuff. No one laughed. The audience was wishing it was over. The lighting tech was trying to figure out when to turn the lights off to signal the end of the scene. And the performers just wanted to get off the stage.

"We want to experience those good scenes again!" the improvisers lamented. "We don't ever want those bad scenes to happen again. What should we do?" Thus, the rules were born and have lived on in improv history ever since. But I love Napier's conclusion about these rules (in his own stream of consciousness kind of way):

"Learning rules can be bad improvisation.

Why, why?

Because the worst part about rules is that people remember them. Often above and beyond anything else. It satisfies and stimulates the left brain. Oh, for a list. "There they are, all numbered and listed. I can remember that. I will remember that. I will remember The Rules of improvisation. How could I not? After all, they are The Rules."

They stick to the brain like glue. They help you think about stuff. Why, you can't help but think about The Rules. They're all memorized in your head. They're "in your head."... The Rules. The Rules. Got 'em all? Think about them because you don't want to break one, think long and hard -

Now, improvise, play!

Good luck.

Yes. That's why I'm not a big fan of The Rules. They help people think in a particular way and that way of thinking is often death to good improvisation. I've watched those damn Rules screw people up for years, and I don't mean that for years, I've seen The Rules screw people up. Individuals who can think of nothing else on stage but The Rules, wandering around powerlessly for years, thinking and measuring and being very careful not to break The Rules, all the while wondering why they are not improving, Improvising.

Left brain, analytical heaven. Not very much fun.

That's religion. We have a great experience with God. We attempt to recreate it. It doesn't turn out the way we expect. We consider it a failure because we didn't find what we were looking for, so we create rules and systems to avert failure in the future. All we want is greater intimacy with God, but in our attempts to control our encounters with Him, we do just the opposite. We stop relying on God and end up confined in a dead religion of rules.

I have a company called Uncover The Color. We create reflective and interactive experiences for conferences and events all over the country. We'll go to a Christian conference (put on by wonderful people and attended by wonderful people) and create an interactive art piece in a worship environment. Some people connect with it. Others simply walk by taking photos with their cell phone cameras thinking, "Ooo. This is cool. I'll take it back and do it at my church, and people will think it's cool." But think about it. Experiences can't be recreated like that. Experiences are all about the uniqueness of a moment and the people who experience it and the context and the momentary movement of God in that place. To take something into a different place at a different time with different people and expect the same result only sets us up to be let down.

But that's what we've done with the Church.

All across the globe, you can walk into a church on a given day and see the same images and videos and hear the same songs and sermons and anticipate the same order and elements of worship. We've settled for re-creation rather than discovering the uniqueness of what God wants to do in and through us at a particular moment in time.

But it's not solely our Sunday worship. No. We've created an entire Christian institution that perpetuates sameness.

And let me pause here and say, I love the Church. The more I love Jesus, the more I love his people. The more I see his deep heart to empower us for the work he wants to accomplish on the earth, the more passionate I feel about doing whatever it takes to bring that to fruition. I'm not a deconstructionist. I don't believe all our systems need to be done away with. I don't hate organization. I believe all things are ripe with the potential for purpose. And this book is—at no point—an excuse for either you or me to bail on the Church.

Instead, it is a call to rethink what it means to follow Jesus, to be the Church, to make ourselves available and willing to express the uniqueness of our personality, our time period, our circumstances, and our community in our church bodies.

I used to hate the suburbs. I grew up there and had fun with my friends—riding go carts around our suburban block, wreaking havoc, and stirring the waters of mischievousness. But eventually, I grew to dislike them. They became a representation of what was wrong with modern, western society. White picket fences were the insurmountable walls that divided one house from another, one family from another, like brothers on opposite sides of the Berlin Wall. I started to see our picket fences as a representation of a culture moving from relationship and interdependence to isolation and aloneness. Then I listened to my friend, Mel, give a talk about architecture and thoughtful, community-centered design. He said he used to hate suburbia, like I did. Then one day, God opened his eyes. He realized every strip mall, each vast expanse of asphalt or row of tract housing, came with a dream, a vision, a light of hope. Now he sees not what's broken, but all that *could* be be in every space, building, and piece of architecture.

This is the way I feel about the Church. I love it. I used to see what was broken. Now I see what it can be.

This mind and spirit shift isn't just about suburbia or the Church. It's a whole new way of seeing. I'll talk about this more in the coming chapters, but right now, let's shift our attention back to what is, where we are, and how we got here. Back to our story.

We have this New Testament Church—the Church of Acts—filled with the Holy Spirit and discovering the depths of God, more and more every day. Somewhere along the way, desperate to recreate the movements of God we heard about in the past, we began creating systems and rules and coming up with formulas. And, what do you know—religion was born.

SPIRITUAL INNOVATION

In the last chapter, we discussed a brief explanation of the Industrial Revolution. Alongside that, more broadly in culture, was the Enlightenment. This era in human history brought us universities, the scientific method and—concurrently in christendom —seminaries.

It was as if to say, to an increasingly intellectual culture, "Oh yeah? God makes sense too. Let me prove it to you." The trouble is, God doesn't make sense. This is by no means an anti-intellectual statement. Rather, a statement about objective. Is the format of our institutions stifling curiosity and a sense of discovery or stimulating it?

That was Jesus' point. I can just imagine Jesus saying, "Adam and Eve tried to figure it out on their own. The religious try to figure it out on their own. You ask me questions. I tell you stories. Because the pursuit of God isn't about trying to figure everything out. The pursuit of God is about the mystery and discovery of relationship. And sure, you learn along the way, but your understanding is not what's most important." Paul, as Paul tended to do, said it even more straightforwardly in 1 Corinthians 2.

Paul begins the chapter by juxtaposing two things: 1) one's ability to convince by means of eloquence and intellect and 2) the good news of Jesus accepted as the result of the demonstration of the Spirit's power. He says he "did not come with eloquence or superior wisdom as [he] proclaimed to [them] the testimony about God." Instead he "came to [the Corinthians] in weakness and fear, and with much trembling." Then Paul points out why. It wasn't because he was inept (although maybe he was). It wasn't because he was afraid (although maybe he was). Paul didn't come with "wise and persuasive words, but with a demonstration of the Spirit's power, so that [their] faith might not rest on men's wisdom, but on God's power."

This stark contrast parallels the contrast we see between the book of Acts and our modern context. Whereas the early church relied on the power of the Holy Spirit to speak to those who's hearts were ripe, most often, our means of evangelism consists of using words or arguments to convince or coerce. But are our wise and persuasive words enough to introduce humanity to an active, powerful God?

Paul goes on,

We do, however, speak a message of wisdom among the mature, but not the wisdom of this age or of the rulers of this age, who are coming to nothing. No, we speak of God's secret wisdom, a wisdom that has been hidden and that God destined for our glory before time began. None of the rulers of this age understood it, for if they had, they would not have crucified the Lord of glory. However, as it is written:

"No eye has seen, no ear has heard, no mind has conceived what God has prepared for those who love him"—

but God has revealed it to us by his Spirit.

The Spirit searches all things, even the deep things of God.
(1 Corinthians 2:6-10)

What Paul is saying here is the Spirit reveals to us the reality of something deeper than the mind. Of course, we have our brains. There's no denying that. And God does not ask us to turn our brains off when coming to Him. But we've done ourselves a disservice in making our brains the primary means by which we approach God. Why, when we want to talk about spiritual things, is our first question most often, "What is God teaching you?"

Doesn't this seem odd? What would your response be if the default question you were asked about your spouse was, "What is your wife/husband teaching you?"

Have we lost the wonder of relationship?

The transition of the Church—from the powerful demonstration of the work of the Holy Spirit to educational institution—has resulted in the demystification and de-romanticization of the Divine relationship God invites us into and ushered us into an era of the systemization of God through intellectualism called theology. We've reduced something meant to be alive and thriving to the study of what was—something in the past. Our relationship with God has been made antiquated, and the only way we can interact with a God of the past is intellectually.

This is where we find ourselves—in a controlled religion of systems that let us know *about* God but never really allow us to *know* him the way we so desperately long to do.

KNOWING DEEPLY

Watchman Nee, a 19th century Chinese pastor, evangelist, and writer wrote about the three components of our humanity as illuminated in scripture in his 1903 book, *The Spiritual Man*. He helped illuminate the unique distinction between body, soul, and spirit. We often recognize the distinction between the physical and metaphysical, but we fail to recognize the difference between soul and spirit.

The body is the physical part of who we are. This is the part of us we can touch and see, the physical matter that comprises our living, breathing bodies. The soul is our character or our persona—the mind, will, and emotions of a person. While these are lived out in the physical and chemical processes of the body and brain, they rest somewhere between the seen and unseen. The original word for this in the Bible is *nephesh* which, when translated into english, reads as "soul, self, life, creature, person, appetite, mind, living being, desire, emotion and passion."

What's important to note about the soul is that it includes the mind and our emotions. In our modern, western context, we often separate these two: mind and emotions. Each of us defaults to trusting one over the other. We either believe we can only trust our logical intuition as solid and concrete, while our emotions should be filtered through intellect before being trusted. Or we trust how we *feel* to determine the direction of our decisions and consider that to be more important than intellect. Rarely do we see the two as working in tandem.

In actuality, *both* our mind and emotions are part of the flesh. We find ourselves creating intellectual constructs to justify how we feel. Then we respond emotionally to the intellectual constructs. Both the mind and emotions are in the cycle of self-reliance—leaning on our own understanding. This is what Nee points out in his analysis of the creation story. Nee says, "Satan gained Adam's will through his emotion and caused him to sin. The way Satan beguiled Eve was to confuse her mind, gain her will, and then cause her to sin."

In other words, Satan convinced Eve through the use of logic to eat from the Tree of the Knowledge of Good and Evil." While Adam was lured through his emotional connection to Eve.

Both the mind and emotions were subject to corruption.

So, if the center of decision-making is not to be the mind or the emotions, how do we operate? This is the role of the spirit in us—the eternal part of who we are is the place where God communicates with us individually. It's the spiritually perceptive piece of each of us that is meant to be the focus of our spiritual lives but is often the least active part of our humanity. When the serpent persuaded Adam and Eve through their mind and emotions, it was their spirit that ultimately suffered.

When man's will, mind, and emotion were poisoned by the serpent to follow Satan and to rebel against God, the spirit with which man communicates with God received a fatal blow. Here we see the principle of Satan's work. He beguiled man's soul to sin through the things of the flesh (the eating of the fruit). Once the soul has sinned, the spirit falls into darkness and degradation. This is the order of all his works—from the outside to the inside. Either he works from man's body or he works from his mind or his emotion for the purpose of gaining his will. Once man's will surrenders, Satan gains the whole being, and the spirit is put to death.

But God builds in the opposite direction.

God's work is always from the inside to the outside. He first works from man's spirit, then enlightens man's mind, touches man's emotion, finally causes man to exercise his will to activate his body to carry out God's will. All the devil's works go from the outside to the inside, while all the works of God's Spirit go from the inside to the outside. In this way we can differentiate what is of God and what is of Satan."

In other words, as we increase in intimacy with God, we learn to hear his voice and discern from a deeply spiritual place.

It's in this working of God from the inside, outward, that we begin to see a re-kindling of how we are meant to live. Not in an attempt to figure everything out on our own but in relying on God to give us supernatural wisdom to make decisions supernaturally. To rely on God is not to shut the mind down but to move into a greater level of effective thinking. Let me explain.

Solomon, the king of Israel, is a blatant example of the power of supernatural thinking. Even in his day, Solomon was known for his wisdom, but he wasn't just a lucky guy with a good head on his shoulders. Solomon made decisions from a place of intimacy with God.

Late one night, as Solomon slept, God came to him and asked,

"What do you want of me?" Solomon's response, "You've given me a big job, and I need wisdom beyond me to accomplish it." Solomon knew that, in order to accomplish the task set before him, he needed something beyond his own human strength and ability. He needed the wisdom of God. He needed ideas beyond what he could imagine in his mind. He needed creativity beyond what he could construct on his own.

And God gave him supernatural wisdom and much more. As Solomon led the people of Israel, he soon developed a reputation throughout the known world as a man who governed with power and wisdom, surpassing any other ruler.

The Queen of Sheba traveled to Israel because she had heard of the wisdom with which Solomon ruled. 1 Kings 10 says, "When the queen of Sheba saw all the wisdom of Solomon and the palace he had built, the food on his table, the seating of his officials, the attending servants in their robes, his cupbearers, and the burnt offerings he made at the temple of the Lord, she was overwhelmed."

Solomon's wisdom wasn't only some spiritual reality. It extended into every aspect of Solomon's rule, including how his servants were dressed and how he set his table. The supernatural wisdom of God flowed through Solomon so that even the most menial tasks were performed with a high level of excellence and wonder.

That's the thing with supernatural wisdom. It not only affects the spiritual realm. It radically shifts the world around us.

Paul, when talking to the Galatians, acknowledged the power of spirit-birthed, inside out living.

... the gospel I preached is not something man made up. I did not receive it from any man, nor was I taught it. Rather, I received it by revelation from Jesus Christ. (Galatians 1:11-12)

SPIRITUAL INNOVATION

The message he preached to them was not derived from the mind or heart. It was derived from a divine, supernatural source, deep in the sprit.

And yet despite this, our contemporary habit resembles the outside-in model, not the inside out model. In our desire to control ourselves, others, and God, we have devised safe, outside-in methodologies that attempt to eliminate risk and systematize the mystical nature of an unending God. It puts control in our hands, just as Adam and Eve desired as they partook of the Tree of the Knowledge of Good and Evil in the Genesis account.

One of the results of our systemization is the vast chasm between what we consider "spiritual" time and the rest of our lives. We may intercede for someone's sickness in the midst of a prayer time at church, but would never consider praying for an ailing stranger on the sidewalk.

One afternoon, my friend Matt told me his wrist hurt. If we were in the safe, controlled environment of "church" I'd pray for healing right away, but there was a tension in me that made me feel awkward about praying for him in the car that day. My friend Nick told me about someone he had been having some rough conversations with. I knew I wanted to pray, but it felt awkward to just break into prayer in the middle of the gym. My friend Esther had an earache. We were both working at a Christian conference—we were the people who were partly leading the event—and still it felt too uncontrollable to break into prayer there in the lobby of the building. Fortunately, in all three of these scenarios I got over my desire for control and the tension of the moment and stepped into prayer.

So what has our desire for control led to? A powerless church—detached from a life-giving, powerful relationship with God. And because God desires to demonstrate His power through His Church, we render God impotent and dead in our own lives and in the world.

So, Nietzsche was right. "God is dead." But not because He is incapable or lacks compassion or is distant. Rather, because His Church has ceased to listen. We've given up God in exchange for something much safer.

QUESTIONS AND CONVERSATIONS :

- Do you seek systems of control in your life in an attempt to minimize risk? Why? What are the things you fear the most and attempt to avoid?

- Throughout this book, there is some talk about improvisation on stage. Imagine yourself doing that. Does that excite you or instill fear? What do you think those feelings reveal about you?

- Do you tend to trust your mind or emotions more? Why? How can you move your life to greater dependence on God in your decision making process?

DO SOMETHING :

Live a moment of improvisation this week. Find a situation to which you would normally say "no" because it makes you uncomfortable and, instead, say "yes." It doesn't have to be an overtly "spiritual" thing. It can be something that makes you face a fear in any area of your life. Learn to be present in that moment with the events and people around you. Ask God for supernatural wisdom as you navigate the situation. Ask Him to help you see how He is moving and how you can participate in it.

SPIRITUAL INNOVATION // CHAPTER THREE
RELIGION AND POLITICS
OUR COMMUNAL NEED FOR CONTROL

SPIRITUAL INNOVATION

Every Christmas growing up, there was a family in my neighborhood who went all out with the decorations and lights on the outside (and probably inside) of their house. The day after Thanksgiving, the switch would be flipped and the house would come alive with light and animated figurines and statues. They would spell out words on their bushes and cover their entire roof with strand after strand of Christmas lights. Every inch of their trees, their grassy lawn, and the low, wooden fence at the edge of their front yard would be transformed into a shimmering source of multi-colored light. Even at 16, when I started driving alone, I can remember going out of my way to drive by the house between Thanksgiving and the New Year, each time I would leave our neighborhood.

I loved it. All the while, the adults in our neighborhood made comments about how tacky the house was. With that in my mind, I was confused as to why I liked this house so much when, apparently, I should think it tacky. It made me uncomfortable. So, in staying true to what I had learned, I decided to criticize it—to come against it—in hopes that it might, somehow, make me feel better.

One afternoon when I was about 12, I convened a posse of guys from the neighborhood and we devised a plan. Together, we walked from my house and around the corner. The combination of knowing I was about to do something deviant and the humidity of the air made my palms sweaty, but we were on a mission and we weren't slowing down. I'm sure we were unnaturally quiet as we walked down the sidewalk—a conspicuous place for five or six preteen boys in a suburban neighborhood with little road traffic. Finally, we reached the shrubs at the edge of the Crazy Christmas House. We looked at each other, slowed our pace slightly, and pulled individual bulbs from the strands of lights on the fence and shrubs at the edge of the property. We knew we were putting entire strands out of commission by such a simple act, and for some reason, we were happy about that.

I loved that house. I enjoyed driving by it, walking by it, riding my bike by it. I would go out of my way to see it. But I attacked it because it was different, and that made people (ultimately me) uncomfortable.

God. Thinking about that now makes me depressed. The thought of a middle-aged man outside his house scanning strands of lights for missing bulbs, replacing them one by one, working to resurrect this thing he cared about and cultivated so much. I can see his face—this man who loved something and was committed to it and gave his time and money to bring it into existence. It didn't matter to him that it was different. It didn't matter to him that other people didn't like it. He knew *he* liked it, he knew it meant something to him, and that was enough.

In Chapter 2, we discovered the need for control in our own lives. In this chapter, we'll discover how that need for control moves beyond individual control and into controlling people institutionally. But for now, let's look at how we live within, contribute to, and create systems of control for ourselves. I believe this will allow us to discover how we can proactively make way for something better.

THE SIMILARITY BETWEEN RELIGION AND POLITICS

Religion and politics are identical twins. Why do I say that? Well, because Jesus did. In Mark 8, Jesus has just fed 4,000 people by miraculously multiplying a few loaves of bread. Jesus and the disciples get on a boat and Jesus warns them, "Be careful. Watch out for the yeast of the Pharisees and that of Herod." The Pharisees, as religious leaders, are representative of religion. Herod, a politician, is representative of politics. And both of them exert control over others through their respective means.

The disciples miss the point and start talking about having no bread. Jesus, in my imagination, roles his eyes before he says, "Why are you talking about having no bread? Do you still not see or understand? Are your hearts hardened?"

Jesus tells the disciples to watch out for the yeast of the Pharisees and of Herod—this thing that is congruent between religion and politics. Notice that Jesus isn't telling them to watch out for the Pharisees and Herod, but the "yeast" of these people—the motivating catalyst inside them.

Yeast is a fungus that is added to dough to make it rise. It is also used in the fermentation of many alcoholic beverages including beer and wine. The people of Jesus' day were familiar with the catalytic properties of yeast and the ability for even a small amount of yeast to permeate the entire batch of whatever it's added to. In Galatians 5:9, Paul says, "A little yeast works through the whole batch of dough." In Matthew 13:33, Jesus says, "The kingdom of heaven is like yeast that a woman took and mixed into about sixty pounds of flour until it worked all through the dough." Whether in reference to sin or the kingdom of heaven or the political or religious spirits, the concept of yeast throughout scripture pertains to its permeating nature, it's ability to affect everything it touches.

In warning his disciples to watch out for the "yeast" of these people instead of warning them of the people themselves, Jesus is warning them not to become *like* the Pharisees and Herod. Jesus points out that we are all tempted and all have the ability to fall into these systems of control over others. It gets into our lives, puffs up, and permeates throughout our whole being.

This yeast was present in the garden of Eden as Adam and Eve attempted to control their own lives by eating of the Tree of Knowledge of Good and Evil. And it continues on until it manifests in the collective outliving of our need for control. The political and religious spirits are the organizational tendency to use tactics of control or domination as a way of forcing others to conform to a certain, man-made image of what they consider right or proper.

RELIGION AND POLITICS

This is the story of the Pharisees. They were men who meant well. They desired to connect people with God. But in so doing, they established a system of rules to regulate the behavior of the people. And soon, things got out of hand. Rules were piled on top of rules. A religious system was born that replaced care for the hearts and lives of people with a set of regulations by which everyone should live. The pharisees were the religious conservatives of their day.

Our tendency is to put these systems of control in the realm of the "powerful people," but we'd be remiss in doing so. These systems scale to our lives everyday. Perhaps it manifests itself in your attempt to control someone else through a passive aggressive comment or action. Or maybe you withhold a compliment in order to make sure someone doesn't get too prideful in your own estimation. Or perhaps you snub someone in an attempt to punish them for what you consider to be inappropriate behavior.

Anytime we attempt to alter someone's behavior by any means other than exhibiting the love and compassion of Christ, we can usually find it rooted in either the political or religious spirit.

Throughout the twentieth century, we've seen an increased entanglement of politics and religion—partially because they have the same end goal (making them perfect candidates for a co-dependent relationship). The 2012 presidential election season, and the fate of Mitt Romney, is a clear example of this partnership.

Growing up, I was part of a church community that literally did a months-long teaching series on various "cults." One of those "cults" we studied was Mormonism. A short, burly man would get up in front of the congregation each Sunday night to talk through the secret documents and traditions of the Church of Jesus Christ of Latter Day Saints. We heard it all—from devout church members one day becoming a ruler of their own planet to the secret, spiritual underwear worn under church members' clothes. Whether or not

SPIRITUAL INNOVATION

Mormonism is a cult, and whether it is part of the Christian Church or not, is moot for this discussion. The point is that this sentiment about the Mormon Church was, at least at that time, generally held by most Evangelicals.

As we'll see in a minute, those ideals get confused when they marry themselves to a political party or political decision. But first, a story:

The year is 2002 and political pundit, Glenn Beck, has rocketed into talk radio success. He moves from a locally produced show based in Tampa to a nationally syndicated spot and quickly gains popularity in conservative (especially conservative Christian) circles. His show is labeled by the New York Times a "mix of moral lessons, outrage, and an apocalyptic view of the future … capturing the feelings of an alienated class of Americans." His popularity grows and he becomes increasingly outspoken about his belief in God and his faith as a Mormon. Beck holds a series of rallies which draw tens of thousands of attendees. And in August 2010, he is a primary speaker and organizer for the Restoring Honor Rally in Washington, DC. Attendance estimates for that event range from 87,000 to 500,000.

It was a day that would do its work to blur the already obscure line between evangelicalism, Christianity, and politics. Conservative op-ed writer for The New York Times, Ross Douthant, wrote, "This was a tent revival crossed with a pep rally intertwined with a history lecture married to a U.S.O. telethon—and that was just in the first hour. There was piety—endless piety, as speaker after speaker demanded that Americans rededicate themselves to God."

While some Evangelical leaders felt it best to steer clear of Beck because of his Mormonism, many defended him. Jerry Fallwell Jr. said, "Glenn Beck's Mormon faith is irrelevant. People of all faiths, all races and all creeds spoke and attended the event. Nobody was there to endorse anyone else's faith, but we were all there to honor our armed forces and to call the people of America to restore honor." (The Salt Lake Tribune)

Bryan Fischer, of the Conservative and Evangelical American Family Association, justified the partnership with Beck by saying, "While Glenn Beck provided the platform, evangelicals provided the message. Beck depended heavily on historian and committed evangelical David Barton for assistance in picking speakers and selecting those who would lead in prayer and worship. A Mormon teed up the ball for Evangelical Protestants. And Evangelicals hit it out of the park." (Christianity Today, 2010)

It was the perfect preamble to Mitt Romney's 2012 Republican Presidential nomination, which received widespread support from the Evangelical community. Hundreds of thousands of Evangelicals had already been conditioned to the idea that Evangelicalism and Mormonism were not incompatible, especially if it meant gaining the high ground morally and politically. Political power and influence, it seems we had decided, would outweigh the means by which it was obtained.

In subsequent chapters of this book, I will celebrate the fusion of the Christian with things we traditionally see as "non-Christian." I will challenge us to a deeper level of engagement with those like us and those unlike us. I don't give this example as a chastisement of the cooperation of evangelicals and Mormons. I give this example to point out its fundamental opposition to evangelical ideals. And, in that philosophical friction, we see religion and politics merging to serve as accomplices in achieving their mutual end goal—control.

The point is this: Evangelicals were willing to go *against* their ideals as long as it meant achieving the results they wanted—the ability to conform others to their moral code through the use of legislation. This is where religion and politics get married and this is where things get really dangerous.

SPIRITUAL INNOVATION

The ultimate result of the unholy union of evangelicalism and politics is not a life change through the person of Jesus. The end result is the imposition of an exterior behavior modification. Remember, this is how satan works—from the outside-in. When we do this, we are not introducing the world to the God of power from the Bible. We are forcing the world to hide themselves behind an exterior of white washed headstones.

There are two results of legislated morality.

1. Hide, then 2. Rebel.

The evangelical church has spent decades dictating rules without engaging in relationship. Collin, a pastor friend of mine, was recently sitting at a table of eight white men in their fifties. They were complaining about "kids these days" and how things were so great "back when I was their age." They were painting an idealized picture of the adolescents of yesteryear and decrying "the mess we're in now." Collin stopped them. "Hold on. You realize you're complaining about the children *you* raised? This is the fruit of *your* life." The perspective these men were taking was to distance themselves from a reality close to them, point at it, and call it broken. That's the posture politicized evangelicalism has taken for decades.

We've made statements, drafted laws, lobbied legislators, created massive organizations to uphold "family values," put bumper stickers on our cars, posted our opinions on the internet and have—all the while—managed to stay at a safe distance from the risk of relationship. We can stand at a distance and yell our viewpoints at people all day long. Social media, a stage, a microphone, a newspaper editorial column—all these things give us the ability to say what we want to say without ever having to interact with those with whom we assume we disagree.

Relationships become a nuisance when our objective is to justify our own viewpoints and create comfortable silos. If this is our ultimate goal, distance is necessary. Relationships change things. In relationship, we discover everyone is an anomaly when we get to know them. Everyone has a story that makes them an exception to our clearly defined inclinations.

When we fail to engage them, those forced outside the realm of acceptance in western, Evangelical culture create new cultures of their own. Thus, a culture war begins. This war doesn't start over ideologies or who's right and who's wrong. It doesn't originate in areas of the intellect. It's a relational war, and it's all in the heart. It's a war that says, "unless you're like me, I can't love you." And thus, the white-washing cycle tumbles on. We persist in our objective of sameness and conformity.

Approach someone who's hurt as the result of rejection and tell them what you think they should do with their life. It doesn't work. All they want to do is hide—or rebel.

This obsession with sameness isn't limited to the attempt to conform individuals to our religious expectations. The desire extends generationally as well. The baby boomers were labeled "the silent generation." They saw themselves as a timid, identity-less generation. Their greatest achievement in their own minds was to replicate the achievements of those who came before them, of those they deemed "the greatest generation." What hope does anyone who follows the "greatest" anything have? And so, they only knew how to live quietly, stagnantly in the shadow of the "greatest generation." And the conformity they had come to believe was best for themselves became what they would believe was best for anyone who came behind them. They developed a worldview of degradation—the world was getting worse, less original, the best was always behind them. They, themselves, being the first copy of the "greatest." And so when their children and their children's children were two and three generations away from the "greatest", they became preservationists. They were warriors in fighting to make things "the way they used to be." Change became the enemy.

Somehow, the Church became the last bastion of what was. We became curators of a museum and God was a relic. The Church became irrelevant, not because it wasn't cool or trendy, but because its purpose was to fight the inevitability of change. Our battles were no longer in the spiritual realm. We put down any weapons of real power and started arguing about whether drums were allowed in the "sanctuary" or whether we should use screens or hymnals. The church became a joke because it *was* a joke.

The world was looking for answers to important questions. The world was busy looking for a cure for cancer. And we were arguing about pews and drums.

THE ROBOT FACTORY

Growing up, I was conditioned to believe that the proper human response to something that made me uncomfortable (anything different than me) was to criticize it. I came to believe criticism was the chief tool by which we passive-aggressively convinced people to conform to our expectations, without saying it outright.

My friend Aradhana, directed a play called "Road to Mecca." At the time, I didn't know anything about the play, but because she directed it, and because our friend Robin played the lead role, I went.

The story opens on an eccentric living room in a small village called Nieu-Bethesda in Eastern Cape, South Africa. The year is 1974. Miss Helen is overwhelmed with excitement by the arrival of an unexpected visitor from the city, Elsa Barlow—the elderly Miss Helen's only friend. Elsa has arrived to help a desperate Miss Helen.

RELIGION AND POLITICS

Since the death of her husband 15 years prior, Helen has embarked on a journey to turn her home into her own personal "Mecca". Over a decade and a half, she has built sculptures depicting scenes from biblical texts and inspired by the poems of Omar Khayyam and literature by William Blake. Using wire, concrete, and finely crushed glass, her house (the Owl House) has been transformed into a glittering wonderland. Miss Helen loves her house so much but it has become the source of disdain for her neighbors. Now, in her old age and without her husband, Miss Helen seems like an easy opponent to defeat.

So the people of Nieu-Bethesda send Rev. Marius Byleveld—the town pastor—to convince Miss Helen to give up the house and move into a group home elsewhere in the village. This proposal, along with Miss Helen's failing eyesight, is the reason Elsa has come.

It's clear, early on, that Elsa won't let Miss Helen be pushed around by the villagers, especially Rev. Marius. When he arrives, the environment is immediately tense. But she is equally as upset with Miss Helen as she is with Rev. Marius. It seems Miss Helen has lost her will to create, to stand out, and ultimately to stand up for herself.

Eventually, Elsa confronts Rev. Marius about an event in which some children came to throw rocks at Miss Helen's house.

Elsa : ... Those children didn't arrive at their attitude to Helen on their own. I've also heard about the parents who frighten naughty children with stories about Miss Helen's "monsters." They got the courage to start throwing stones because of what they had heard their mothers and fathers saying. And as far at *they* are concerned, Helen is anything but a harmless old lady. God, what an irony. We spend our time talking about "poor, frightened Miss Helen," whereas it's all of you who are really frightened.

Marius : I can only repeat what I've already said to Helen: the people

SPIRITUAL INNOVATION

you are talking about grew up with her and have known her a lot longer than you.

Elsa : Not anymore. You also said that, remember? That stopped fifteen years ago. When she didn't resign herself to being the meek, churchgoing little widow you all expected her to be. Instead she did something which small minds and small souls can never forgive... she dared to be different! Which does make you right about one thing, Dominee [Marius]. Those statues out there *are* monsters. And they are that for the simple reason that they express Helen's freedom. Yes, I never thought it was a word you would like. I'm sure it ranks as a cardinal sin in these parts. A free woman! God forgive us!

In that moment, sitting in that theater, I shuddered and put my head down. I was reminded of that story from my own life from the beginning of this chapter. I pictured that man who loved his Christmas lights checking the strands, socket after socket, looking for the missing bulbs my friends and I had pulled out. His only crime was this: caring about something. In cultivating that thing well, he became an outcast, simply because he was different.

These days, I'm at a place in my life where I'm constantly doing things that are seen by people: art, speaking, writing, music. So much of what I do through my art is celebrating things that are "different"—challenging people to get outside of themselves, to take risks—and more often than not that means I'm trying to lead by example. Being an artist means being different. Being different means being seen. Being seen means being positioned for more and more criticism.

Being an artist (or doing anything important) means being Miss Helen or the owner of the Crazy Christmas House. You stand out. And standing out makes a lot of people uncomfortable.

In the book of Luke, Jesus says there are those who "... by persevering produce a crop." I think Jesus was a lot like Miss Helen and the Christmas light family. He said a lot of things that made people who followed the established way of being and thinking really uncomfortable. At the end of his life, Jesus, like Miss Helen, felt all alone. But they both pressed on doing what they knew they were supposed to do. They didn't let the rock-throwers or the whispers of the villagers or the finger shaking of the establishment stop them. They persevered.

So what does this have to do with religion and politics? Religion and politics necessitate and work toward sameness. They are the vessels in our culture by which individuals are amassed and corralled into conformity—whether for the sake of convenience or because of the fact that "different" often means uncomfortable.

Look at our current political reality. As the United States becomes increasingly influenced by a political spirit, we see a polarization based on firmly held philosophical differences. And while the two sides are growing ever distant and divided, the two sides are more homogeneous than ever. Our political system has been reduced to two hyperbolized caricatures, and we as individuals are expected to align completely with one side or the other. Sameness.

And even as wider culture and politics are changing, western Christianity and the way it manifests itself is changing as well. Evangelicalism is becoming the politicized, western counterfeit of following Christ. It's time for things to change. Don't you think?

EVANGELICAL EVANGELISM

I've grown up as part of the American Evangelical church. It wasn't until I started writing this book that I realized:

American Evangelicalism does not equal following Christ. In fact, people were following Christ long before America or Evangelicalism and people will be following Christ long after both cease to exist.

It seems like such a simple reality, but—depending on your experience—it might sound completely heretical. That's because those who have grown up in the institution of Christianity have been led to believe the two are synonymous—that the depiction of "Christ-follower" in contemporary American culture is the only and ultimate depiction of Christ-follower. And yet to say the two are the same is to say there were no Christians before American Evangelicalism, which, I hope we can agree, is certainly not the case.

So where's the dividing line? It rests in answering the question: "What's Jesus and what's not?"

To answer this question, we can look to The Pharisees, who were excellent at having good intentions and yet suffered some dire and unexpected consequences. Their hope was to please God. In their understanding, all the systems and rules they were creating were "biblically based" as the term goes. They figured out systems by which they could instruct people to live so they might avoid making God mad. And as a result, they loved sameness. They cherished conformity. It was easy to target those who were displeasing God, because those people were different. When everything is the same and one thing is different, the different thing stands out. Sound familiar?

This disease of sameness defines Evangelical culture. Here's a simple example: a bookshelf. If you have a certain book on your shelf, you're giving that book an endorsement of sorts. When someone looks at your bookshelf, they can get an idea of the types of things you've read and researched. That's why one of the books on my shelf has a white piece of paper around the binding. I pulled the book from the shelf and found it, ironically, placed between Ayn Rand's "Anthem" and Orwell's "1984." I bought the book as a 16-year-old.

An (unnamed) guy wrote this (to remain unnamed) book in the late nineties and every youth pastor thought it important for every boy in his youth group to read. The book paints this very American Evangelical idea of what it means to be a man, then tries to create a spiritual framework for that idea. The author writes in hopes of creating sameness among the men of our species. In the second chapter, the author is asking what Jesus is like.

"Isn't he sort of meek and mild?" a friend remarked. "I mean the pictures I have of him show a gentle guy with children all around. Kind of like Mother Theresa." Yes, those are the pictures I've seen myself in many churches. In fact, those are the only pictures I've seen of Jesus. As I've said before, they leave me with the impression that he was the world's nicest guy. Mister Rogers with a beard. Telling me to be like him feels like telling me to go limp and passive. Be nice. Be swell. Be like Mother Theresa.

I'd much rather be told to be like William Wallace.

I've never had a conversation with the guy who wrote this book. I'm sure, like the Pharisees, as we all do (myself included), he had good intentions. And while the word "masculine" never appears in the Bible, I'm sure we can say it was this author's desire to write a biblically-based book. And yet, I can't help but feel like his perspective has been influenced by *culture* as much as it has by Christ.

I love risk. I love stepping out in faith. I love doing things simply because they make me feel alive. And I believe those things are central to abundant life in Christ. But then creeps in this American Evangelical stereotype of loving sports and craving violence. He tells boys there's something wrong with them if they don't fit this mold. A couple chapters later, the author writes,

"This is why my boys love to wrestle with me—why any healthy boy wants the same with his father."

SPIRITUAL INNOVATION

Is it possible a man could be a man and not want to wrestle with his father? Is it possible we're not all the same?

Most of my male friends make music and films and paintings. They're artists. A few of them like UFC and Crossfit and shooting guns, and we're still friends, but a lot of them don't do any of those things. Fortunately, we've found a home with one another—a home that says, "I'll meet you where you are and Christ is the foundation for us. That's enough. You don't have to be the same as me. You don't have to like the things I like. You don't even have to believe the things I believe. You are a human. God loves you. You're valuable. I want you to thrive in the uniqueness of who you are."

There's a distinction between what's Christ-like and what's American, Southern, Evangelical. Regardless of who you are, what your gender is or what you pursue, Christ calls us to a life of risk. Christ calls us to know his love so fully—so deeply—that we're willing to step out in faith. God desires for us to live a life of power and effectiveness and adventure but those things are far removed from the American, Evangelical construct of sameness, of saying that being a man means embracing fighting and guns and war and sports. It's okay to not adopt those things for our lives because they aren't inherent in what it means to be a "Christian." They are cultural.

And we don't only confuse Culture and Christ here at home. Our global reach has been tainted by the confusion as well. It's one of the primary contributors to robbing entire cultures of their ways of life, their celebrations and their traditions.

In my early twenties I took a mission trip to a foreign country. It was an amazing experience—the first time I had an opportunity to be immersed in the Spanish language and utilize my four years of high school Spanish language education. I was there with about 50 other Americans in a small village, centered around a school and church, on the edge of a hill. It was a beautiful time with beautiful people.

Then came the Sunday morning worship gathering. The morning we were there, an American gave a sermon that was translated into Spanish by one of the local missionaries. Then came a time of music. The songs were oddly familiar melodically and I knew enough spanish to recognize we were singing American worship songs translated into spanish. This church—being technologically advanced—also projected the words on a pulldown screen from an old laptop, using powerpoint. The presentation had brightly colored backgrounds and even more brightly colored text. And there, on the side of the lyrics, was a strategically placed animated gif of Dino the Dinosaur from the Flintstones. The purple dinosaur was either dancing or trying to break boards, ninja style.

I'm sure the missionaries who first arrived to this village were well-intentioned. I'm sure their desire was to introduce the people of the village to Christ. But somewhere along the way, Christ got confused with American Evangelicalism—and the worship gathering, had there not been a spanish translator, could have taken place in any small American Evangelical church.

A few years later, I went to Thailand to lead worship for the International Mission Board's Southeast Asia Missionary Conference. It was there I met some young Christians living in India. They were asking great questions and seeing powerful things in the communities where they lived. Several of these young, American missionaries were musicians and had been connecting with the musicians in their villages. In India, there are sacred songs called Bhajans. These songs use traditional stringed, rhythmic instruments and are sung in traditional Indian scales—with quarter tones and intricate flourishes. Bhajans are also sometimes kirtans, a call-and-response type of singing where a leader sings a line and the congregation sings in response.

Being traditionally Indian, this type of devotional singing had found its roots in Hinduism. As a result, many American missionaries rejected not only the lyrical content, but the very style of music, instrumentation, and singing. There was some fear that, even if new songs were written in worship of Yahweh, the use of the traditional scales and styles would be a form of syncretism (the intermeshing of multiple, often conflicting, ideologies). There was a belief by some that, inherent in the intervals between pitches, melodies, rhythms, and styles were aspects beyond the scope of God's redeeming power.

This leaning toward sameness in the area of music isn't only American or Evangelical but it is consistently born under the influence of religiosity. The imposition of musical rules and the belief that certain musical intervals have innate demonic or impure properties dates back at least to the middle ages when the Catholic Church officially rejected the use of the tritone—two notes spanning six half steps. The notes F and B are an example of a tritone. So, in medieval Europe, the Catholic Church would have banned the song "Maria" from the musical "West Side Story" as well as The Simpson's Theme song, both of which begin with a tritone.

Whether it's the tritone or bhajans (or that devil music with those drums and electric guitars), time has shown us what we have failed to see before: our musical rules and expectations aren't birthed from a divine mandate. Rather, they are birthed out of our desire for sameness, which manifests itself in an evil fear of the unknown.

THE FEAR OF THE UNKNOWN

In 1913, a young composer named Igor Stravinsky was commissioned to compose music for the 1913 Paris season of the Ballets Russes. The season was to be held at Paris's Théâtre des Champs-Élysées. Construction was hurried to be ready in time for the opening. The theater held it's inaugural concert on April 2, 1913, and just over a month later, the stage was set for the premiere of Stravinsky's Rite of Spring.

The hall was full that night. Reporter, Gustav Linor wrote, "Never... has the hall been so full, or so resplendent; the stairways and the corridors were crowded with spectators eager to see and to hear." (Kelly, p304, quoting Gustav Linor writing in Comoedia, May 30, 1913, At the Théâtre des Champs-Elysées: Le Sacre du Printemps)

But it wasn't only seeing and hearing that would take place this night. The orchestra got in place, the crowd hushed, and out of the silence, was heard a single bassoon. It was as if the sun was rising over a peaceful field on a calm, warm morning. Soon, other instruments joined the waking composition. Suddenly, the horns and strings started in with a superimposed e-flat triad that continued to pulsate on and off for the duration of the piece. It was an onslaught of sound—one quite unfamiliar to those attending the performance that night, whose ears were more acquainted with the traditional melodies, harmonies, and rhythms of classical music.

The crowd began to shift in their seats, looking at one another with surprise and discomfort. Growing frustrated, Stravinsky moved from the theater seats to the wings of the stage. The roar of the crowd grew louder—so loud the dancers on stage were unable to hear the orchestra. The choreographer stood at the edge of the stage, shouting the counts for the music, "One, Two, Three..." The crowd stood and began throwing things at the orchestra, but they played on. And in a moment of fury, the crowd turned on one another. A riot broke out resulting in 40 members of the crowd being ejected. Eventually the violence subsided.

The remaining performances of the Rite of Spring were well attended, and the crowds were a bit more docile—although tension still existed in the air. But here's the irony in this story. I first heard of this account of the Rite of Spring on NPR's RadioLab. At the end of the segment, they pointed out that the Rite of Spring is included in the animated film, Fantasia, produced by Walt Disney. Only 37 years after the composition caused a riot, it was included in an animated

SPIRITUAL INNOVATION

film suited for children.

In much the same way, aversion to the tritone is passé and arguments about drums only take place in the most rural parts of the world. The sounds themselves haven't changed. The tritone intervals are still the same. The instrumentation and composition of the Rite of Spring are no different. Rather, our ears have adopted the ability to hear the beauty in what was once considered an abomination. The beauty was there all along. We're the ones who have changed.

It has nothing to do with compromise. It has everything to do with growth.

And that's one of the greatest dangers of the conservative pursuit of sameness—stunted growth. Because when we're unwilling to change, it might seem to keep us safe, but what it actually does is prevent us from growing. Risk and growth are integrally connected, and for us to be people of risk, we must be people who are deeply rooted in the uniqueness of our identity.

When we understand the beauty of innovation in the spiritual realm, we recognize you can still follow Jesus and be an individual. In fact, stepping into life with Jesus makes us more *us* than we've ever been before.

QUESTIONS AND CONVERSATIONS:

- How have you noticed the religious and political spirits in your own life? How have you sought to control others (whether a large number of people or a single individual)? Why?

- How have you felt oppressed by the systems around you? Have you been in systems that have sought to control you or make you just like the people around you? How did you respond? Do any of those experiences still affect the way you approach people or systems? How?

- Have you ever been afraid to state your opinion because it was different than the opinion of those around you? How can you humbly and gently step into a place of bravery?

DO SOMETHING :

The Crazy Christmas House guy, Miss Helen and Igor Stravinsky were all pressing the boundaries of what was acceptable, and their eccentricity sometimes made others around them uncomfortable. Press a boundary in a healthy way this week. Be willing to put your reputation on the line for something you think is important.

just like the people around you? How do you feel about some of those statements that affect the way [...] system [...]?

Have you ever been afraid to state your opinion because it was different or things a point [...] nurse and family [...]

Dr. Shah:

First of all, for starters,

SPIRITUAL INNOVATION // CHAPTER FOUR
BREAKING FREE FROM CONTROL

SPIRITUAL INNOVATION

What does it mean when I say that stepping into a life with Jesus makes us more "us" than we've ever been before?

I was teaching an acting class called "Be Present: The Intersection of Faith and the Arts." It was only week two, and already we were getting into some pretty deep things. Most beginning actors spend their time on stage or in front of the camera playing emotions. "Okay, I'm going to be mad in this scene." Or "This character is obviously sad. I'll try to be sad now." You may not know it, but when you think, "Man, she's a bad actor," chances are she's trying to play emotions in a scene.

So, it was only week two of the acting class and we were looking at the reality that, to move from being a mediocre actor to great actor, we don't just play emotions, we have to *become* people who are living out objectives in relationship. But what does this mean? One way to do this is to use verbs to explain what you're trying to do. For example, "I want to belittle my scene partner" or "I want to romance my scene partner" or "I want to cajole my scene partner". The objective is to "be present" and honest in relationship with another living, breathing human being.

Why is that important? Why does it make a difference? Because being in the moment and living an action moves the actor from trying to play a character to actually becoming that character. It moves the actor from pretending to be someone or something to actually embodying the role he or she is playing. And what we believe about ourselves makes a difference in what we do and how we live.

There's an acting coach (although she wouldn't apply that term to herself) named Margie Haber. Part of her philosophy in teaching actors is helping them take on a new vocabulary and, thusly, helping them become more effective at what they do. One of the vocabulary changes is: instead of calling a moment on stage a "scene," she will have her students use the term "slice of life." At one of her workshops, I heard her say, "If you have 30 auditions, you don't have 30 characters to play. You have 30 people to become." It moves the actor from a place of playing a role to a place of knowing who he or she is in each circumstance. It calls that actor to authentically become each character.

Do you see the connection I'm making here? The things that make us uniquely us are as follows: action and authenticity. Without these two things, how do we know who or what we are?

One day in my "Be Present" class we were playing with this concept. I had given each student a verb and they were supposed to act out the verb in their little slice of life. One of the guys in my class, Eric, had been given the verb, "intimidate." He sat across from his scene partner as the rest of the class watched. He spoke a few lines of dialogue with the verb "intimidate" in mind. After he had done that, I asked his scene partner what he felt.

"Eh, not much. He seems mad, but I don't really feel intimidated."

"Alright, one more time, Eric. Let's frame this. Your scene partner has just come over to your house and threatened your wife, and you want to make sure that never happens again."

Eric did the scene two more times, and each time, there was an increased level of tension in the room as Eric became increasingly more intimidating.

In our discussion at the end of the exercise, Eric said, "You know... what someone believes about himself or herself really makes a difference in how effectively they'll live out an action." It's moments like those that make me wish every Christian—every human being—would take a legit acting class.

The goal of following Christ is not to put on a character. It's not to change our behavior or to pretend to be someone else. It's to actually step into a place of renewed identity. It's to know who God says we are. It's to come to a more clear vision of our identity in Christ and to live into the fullness of that identity.

Following Christ is more about who we really are than who we pretend to be.

I never used to think twice when I'd hear a Christian define themselves as a "sinner." I wouldn't bat an eye at the suggestion we're "just broken people", or "that's what it means to be human". But these days, when I hear that rhetoric, I can't help but think about how much time and energy we spend creating systems and theologies that simply justify and perpetuate our pain and depression. We're not broken people who are putting on Jesus. He's made us a new creation. We're not pretending to be like Christ. We actually are like Him. We're not powerless against the things that plague us. We have power to overcome them.

It's becoming less and less cool to smoke, but there are the vestiges of the smoking class still among us… and Lord knows "Mad Men" hasn't helped. What I'm about to say isn't to rail against smoking. No point in that. It's about identity.

A smoker comes to a place in his life where he decides to quit. "I don't want this anymore. It costs me money. It makes me smell like cigarettes. It's killing me. I'm done," he declares one morning before leaving for work. He goes to his bedside table, picks up the pack of cigarettes, breaks them all in half and throws them in the garbage.

He leaves for work, and on the way, remembers he has a spare pack of cigarettes in the glove box. The craving is there, as it is most mornings, but he's resolved that "this time, it's for real. I'm done with this." His will, in this moment, is strong enough to resist the long-developed habit that has been chemically reinforced in his brain and body several times a day for years.

He arrives at work and the busyness of the office takes his mind off the craving for a couple hours. Then, the lunch break comes.

(Sidebar: I'm writing this in a park. A man just stood downwind of me and lit up. That thing I wrote before, "What I'm about to say isn't to rail against smoking. No point in that." I take it back. Please stop. For the sake of all that is good and lovely, please stop.)

Where were we? Right... lunch break.

Smoker Joe, we'll call him. Joe gets back in his car to go meet some friends for lunch, and on the way, he remembers the pack of cigarettes in his glove box. He takes a deep breath, reaches across the center console, puts his finger under the release latch...

And here, we hit the pause button to ask an important question. Does what Joe believes about himself matter in this moment? Does his identity play a role in his decision making process? Do the words he uses to define himself influence his decision? Let's play "choose your own adventure."

In scenario one, we have the events listed above and as Joe slides his finger under the glove box latch, he slowly shakes his head back and forth and declares, "Eh, I'm just a lowly sinner."

In scenario two, Joe slides his finger under the latch, shakes his head vigorously and in a triumphant voice shouts at the top of his lungs, "I am more than a conqueror. I am a beloved child of the King. I am in Christ and seated at the right hand of God! I have been given the keys to the kingdom of heaven, and have been raised into a life of power!"

The story continues on.

SPIRITUAL INNOVATION

Scenario 1

"Eh, I'm just a lowly sinner."

Joe opens the glove box, pulls out the pack of cigarettes. He looks at the cool camel on the box, and knows the entire thing is meant to convince him to have a certain self-identity associated with smoking. He's watched the documentaries about the subliminal objectives of advertising. He remembers that day in middle school when he smoked with his friends for the first time. He sees right through it all. He's completely conscious of the chemical reactions happening in his brain in this exact moment. He even feels a little bit silly about the triviality of the entire situation, but he opens the pack, puts a cigarette between his lips and pulls out the lighter. He feels a bit defeated, yet relaxed, as he breathes deeply and the warm smoke fills his lungs. He holds it in for a moment then slowly exhales the smoke out the window of his car. The smoke quickly dissipates in the wind rushing by the car.

He gets to the restaurant where some of his friends are already waiting out front. He smiles and confesses, "today was going to be the day I quit... again." They all chuckle. Joe smiles and they walk inside.

Scenario 2

"I'm more than a conqueror."

For a moment, Joe pulls his finger off the latch and sits up in the driver's seat. He takes a deep breath, wondering if this is all really that big of a deal, and certainly feeling like it's not really worth the fight. But he makes it to the restaurant. He enjoys lunch with a few friends. They know what it's like. They've all tried to quit at least once—with varying degrees of success. They wish him luck, genuinely.

Joe gets back into his car after lunch. Smoking after lunch is more

Pavlovian than any other time. He bangs the steering wheel. "F$%@#!" he yells, surprising himself. He smokes but he's not usually the cursing type. He shakes his head back and forth, the same way he does when trying not to fall asleep on a long road trip. "This sucks!" He says. "Ahhh!" He quickly reaches over and pulls the latch. The glove box falls open. He grabs the pack of cigarettes and chants "more than a conqueror" repetitiously as the white box of satisfying goodness crosses in front of his face and out the window. He laughs at himself, "Great. Now I'm chanting silly mantras like some western, hippie-bearded Dalai Lama. And I'm littering."

The rest of the work day is rather laborious. He sees a few of his co-workers passing back and forth in front of his desk on their way to and from their smoke breaks. The sweet remnants of smokey goodness waft from their clothes, like the smell of apple pie emanating from his mom's warm oven or the scent of the bread factory he passes on the highway to and from work every day. On the way home, he remembers, smartly, that he didn't flush the cigarettes down the toilet that morning. He just broke them in half and threw them in the trash can in his bedroom. "Ah, I'll fish those little brown shavings out of the trash when I get home. I know I have some wrapping papers laying around somewhere." Then he catches his lips moving. "More than a conqueror. More than a conqueror." He's unsure of whether this latest attempt at cessation is turning him into a Buddhist, chanting mantras.

He texts his girlfriend, Hanna. "Listen babe. This is ridiculous. I need you to meet me at my house. I'm on my way home from work. I'll be there in 15 minutes."

"Is everything okay?"

"With us, yes. But I need your help getting rid of something."

"Dead body?"

"Eh. Kinda."

"Love it. See you soon."

Mind over matter? Nope.

Then what?

New mind, new heart over matter.

Obviously, taking on a God-aligned view of our identity is not a magic potion for all that ails us. In these two scenarios, Scenario 2 is, in all reality, way more difficult than Scenario 1. The story is twice the length and it's just the beginning of a life-long journey. But does Joe's understanding of his identity make a difference? You bet.

What you believe about who you are plays a huge role in defining your attitudes, actions, and circumstances.

Whether it's breaking free from an addiction, developing healthy relationships with others, or accomplishing the dreams you and God have for your life—it's all influenced by what we believe about who we are.

Have you thought about who you are? I don't mean Meyer-Briggs personality test. I'm not talking about "What I want to be when I grow up." I'm asking, "Have you really thought about what you think about who you are when you look in the mirror?" Have you taken inventory of the words you use to describe yourself on a daily basis—both positive and negative? What is your identity? How do you see yourself? Where does your identity come from? And how has it shaped how you see yourself?

Close (or turn off) the book for a little while. Go get quiet. And consider: "Who am I?"

JESUS AND IDENTITY

Jesus was an expert at identity. He knew who he was as a human. He knew who he was in the spiritual realm. He knew who others were and He knew his relationship to them. When we look to Jesus to see how he discovered his identity and why it mattered so much to him, we have a lot to learn about our own identity and how understanding it can allow us to become more like Christ.

John the Baptist, upon seeing Jesus, made a declaration about his identity: "Look, the Lamb of God, who takes away the sin of the world!" (John 1:29). Jesus then went to John and asked to be baptized. It's as if Jesus was saying, "Yes, you know who I am. Will you be the one to confirm that identity in a public space?" As Jesus came up from the water, the Holy Spirit descended on him, and a voice was heard saying, "This is my Son, whom I love; with him I am well pleased."

These were public declarations of what Jesus already knew about himself. They were his identity spoken aloud. In John 8:14 Jesus says, "Even if I testify on my own behalf, my testimony is valid, for I know where I came from and where I am going. But you have no idea where I come from or where I am going."

But it wasn't only Jesus who knew the importance of his identity. So too did the enemy.

After being baptized, Jesus was led out into the wilderness by the Holy Spirit. There, he was tempted.

The first two temptations began with the statement, "if you are the Son of God..." The tactic of the devil was to get Jesus to question his identity. The enemy knew if he could convince Jesus he was something other than who the Father declared him to be, he could get him to succumb to temptation.

That's why knowing who we are is so important. When we know who we are, we live into that identity. Jesus made choices that were in line with his identity.

But where did Jesus' identity come from? Sure, it was declared that day when he was baptized in the river, but Jesus knew who he was long before that day in the river. Jesus' understanding of his identity was directly connected to his deep level of intimacy with God. It was in those moments, when Jesus would slip away to be with the Father in private, that he maintained the intimacy and it spilled over into his public life. Jesus' identity was instilled in private and it made him effective in public.

Knowing his identity was a key factor in the fruitfulness of Jesus' ministry. Jesus lived in such intimacy with the Father, he was able to see what God was doing and join him in that work. And as a result of that intimacy, Jesus' ministry was powerful and effective as he manifested the kingdom realities of love, hope, healing, life and resurrection in the world around him.

So, who does God say we are?

A GOD POINT OF VIEW

This whole identity journey was, for me, rather surprising. I was seeing so many depressed, immobilized people around me and I really believed it had something to do with our identity. So I decided to start a gathering of guys called, "Received As Sons." I wasn't sure what the content of the group would end up being, but I knew it was something we could suss out together. Early in our gatherings, I said, "Okay, we're going to compile a list of who God says we are in Christ. This week, as you read the Bible, write down a list of words used to describe people who are positioned in Christ."

The week went by, and I was already surprised at what I was seeing. I was reading Ephesians that week, and I started compiling this list of words Paul uses to address and identify the Christians living in Ephesus.

Saints	*Predestined*	*Lavished*	*Included*
Faithful	*Adopted*	*Recipients*	*Saved*
Blessed	*Sons*	*Together*	*Sealed*
Chosen	*Gifted*	*In Him*	*Heirs*
Holy	*Redeemed*	*Purposed*	
Blameless	*Forgiven*	*Offerings*	

And that's just in the first 14 verses of Chapter 1! What a contrasting picture to how I so often viewed myself and others as "broken" or "sinner" or "worthless". In fact, what we discovered through our study is that—in using those terms to define ourselves—we were negating the saving work of Christ on the cross and the power of the resurrection. We were reclaiming our old identity rather than living in the new one He granted us in Christ.

Later, we came to Galatians 5:1-2 in which Paul points out the travails of trying to hold on to the old identity.

It is for freedom that Christ has set us free. Stand firm, then, and do not let yourselves be burdened again by a yoke of slavery.

Mark my words! I, Paul, tell you that if you let yourselves be circumcised, Christ will be of no value to you at all.

SPIRITUAL INNOVATION

He goes on in this same chapter to give two lists. One of them is famous—the fruit of the spirit: love, joy, peace, patience, kindness, goodness, faithfulness, gentleness and self-control. The other is less famous: sexual immorality, impurity and debauchery; idolatry and witchcraft; hatred, discord, jealousy, fits of rage, selfish ambition, dissensions, factions and envy; drunkenness, orgies, and the like.

And everyday, the way we define ourselves determines which list we will be prone to live. By defining ourselves as "sinners" we separate ourselves from the person of Christ, reduce our existence to the extent of our fleshly humanity, and willingly accept for ourselves that nature. But by embracing life in the Spirit and the reality of our identity in Christ, we step into a whole new level of expectation for our lives. We move from trying to dig ourselves out of a pit of sin into accepting the grandeur of the life we have in Christ. We no longer see our lives on a scale of negative ten to zero but on a scale of zero to plus infinity. We live in the clean slate, proactive life of fruit-bearing.

When we understand our identity in Christ, we are no longer are fighting to be good enough. Rather, we see who God says we are, we live into that identity, and we step into a greater habit of making decisions in alignment with that identity. This is not just in a moralistic sense of "right" and "wrong." We start making decisions that bring life to ourselves and to those around us. We come into an understanding of the power that lies deep within us to shift environments and bring new life and healing.

Imagine a life freed from trying to please God, freed from the fear of "messing up." Imagine being thrust into a life that brings love where there is not love and peace where there is not peace. In understanding our identity, in light of what Christ has accomplished, we move from trying to earn God's favor to operating in the blessings that already exist for us.

The New Testament is full of these descriptions of who God says we are. Paul, in his letter to the Ephesians, once again contrasts the old life and the new life, life before Jesus and life in him. Before Christ, Paul points out that:

"Like the rest, we were by nature objects of wrath." (Ephesians 2:3)

While so many of us fight to retain the comfortable nature of our old selves, Paul uses the verb "were" and includes a huge "but" after this statement:

But because of his great love for us, God, who is rich in mercy, made us alive with Christ even when we were dead in transgressions—it is by grace you have been saved.

"Ah. Sure." You might say. "Of course. I understand I'm saved by grace. I understand Jesus made a way for my salvation. I get that. BUT... I'm still human. I'm still a sinner. I'm still broken." On the contrary. Not only does Paul point out the reality that we are no longer objects of wrath because of God's grace demonstrated in the person of Jesus, Paul also paints a new picture of our identity, posture, position, and authority:

And God raised us up with Christ and seated us with him in the heavenly realms in Christ Jesus, in order that in the coming ages he might show the incomparable riches of his grace, expressed in his kindness to us in Christ Jesus.

There's so much talk about being "crucified with Christ." There's far less talk about being raised up again. But look at what Paul is saying here. You and I, right now, in our human state, are positioned in Christ. That means, when God looks at you and me, he doesn't see sin. He doesn't see broken. He's not reviled by some stained heart or blotted soul. When God looks at you and me, he sees Jesus. He's not pointing at us, shaking his finger at who we aren't. He's filled with joy and satisfaction by who He's allowed us to be by sending His son, Jesus, to pay the penalty for every wrong, broken mistake we have ever made or ever will make. That's why Jesus, when he breathed his last breath said, "it is finished." That's why Paul, in his letter to the Thessalonians, wrote, "For God did not appoint us to suffer wrath but to receive salvation through our Lord Jesus Christ."

And not only are we in Christ, but we are seated with the Father in the heavenly realms. Just what does this mean? In scripture, there are three uses of the word heaven. The first use is in reference to the earthly realm—the physical space of atoms and elements. "In the beginning, God created the *heavens* and the earth" kind of heaven. In Psalm 19, David pens "The heavens declare the glory of God; and the firmament shows His handiwork." That is referring to the physical spaces our flesh inhabits.

The second type of heaven is the spiritual reality that exists around us. It's the realm of spiritual battle referred to in Ephesians 6:

For our struggle is not against flesh and blood, but against the rulers, against the authorities, against the powers of this dark world and against the spiritual forces of evil in the heavenly realms.

And the third heaven is what we see here—the throne room of God. This is a place of position, of spiritual authority. It's a place above all other realms—maybe not in terms of physical, spatial relationship but certainly in terms of spiritual authority. In 2 Corinthians, Paul talks about a man he knew who was "caught up to the third heaven" where "he heard inexpressible things, things that man is not permitted to tell." *This* is the place in which you and I are seated. Can you believe that? Of course, our bodies are present in the first heaven, but, in Christ, our spirits are seated in the heavenly realms. And because we are positioned there, it gives us authority in the first and second realms. That's why the gates of hell will not prevail against the Church. Because the Church, seated in the third heaven with

God, has dominion and authority over the second heaven, in which spiritual battle ensues. Additionally, being seated in the third heaven gives those who are in Christ's authority in the first heaven—the earthly space. That's why Romans tells us that all creation longs for the revelation of the sons of God. Because those sons of God have heavenly authority to bring about the fullness of the kingdom in the realm of physical existence.

Jesus, in talking about our identity says, "I no longer call you servants, because a servant does not know his master's business. Instead, I have called you friends, for everything I learned from my Father I have made known to you." And Paul, in Galatians 4 says, "So you are no longer a slave, but a son; and since you are a son, God has made you also an heir."

We're not lowly servants in the courts of King God. We're sons and daughters. We're legal heirs to everything that is His—which is everything.

We know the story of the Prodigal son, in which a son asks his father to give him his portion of his inheritance and subsequently went away and squandered it. But the greatest tragedy of the Prodigal son isn't that he ran from the father. It's that he settled for a portion of his father's possessions when he already had access to everything the father had. In consoling the eldest son, the father says, "My son... you are always with me and everything I have is yours."

So, if we have all this authority and position, why do we fight to retain our old identity? Because it's comfortable, it's familiar, and it certainly requires much less from God and from us.

If we serve a powerless God, we don't expect anything from Him. If we don't expect anything from Him, we certainly don't expect anything from ourselves. But if God is who He says He is, and if you and I are who He says we are, then everything has to be different. We approach our world, our circumstances and our relationships with a completely different set of expectations. If God is powerful, and if we're His empowered children, we have the ability to change the state of the world around us—personally, communally, and globally.

Having a clear view of our identity in Jesus thrusts us into a different way of living. We no longer believe we are powerless in a sinful world. Rather, we know we have power to shift reality because of our position in Him.

QUESTIONS AND CONVERSATIONS :

- Who do you say you are? What words do you use to define yourself? Who does God say you are? What words does God use to define you? How are those different? How are they the same? How can you shift into greater alignment with who God says you are?

- Are there actions or habits in your life that could be tied to the way you view your identity? What are they? What do those actions or habits say about what you believe about your identity?

- How does your view of your identity shape the expectations you have for your faith?

DO SOMETHING :

Sit with a trusted friend–someone you consider to have a high level of discernment about people. Ask them what words they would use to describe you. Positive and negative. Later, take those before the Lord and ask for discernment and wisdom about what they said. Ask for wisdom about which words to embrace and which words to release. Then, consider if there are any changes you can implement in your life to continue to step into a greater level of refinement in becoming who you're created to be.

SPIRITUAL INNOVATION // CHAPTER FIVE
THE END OF DOOMSDAY THINKING

Our understanding of identity not only shapes how we see ourselves. It shapes how we see the world and it shapes our understanding of the role we play in in it.

As a middle schooler, I was on the track team. I wasn't fast, but the graciousness of middle school instructors leads them to invite everyone to join, so I was in. In the afternoons, I would often run around the block in our suburban Orlando neighborhood to "train." One afternoon, as I was nearing the end of my run, I saw my brother and one of his friends off in the distance on their bicycles. As my brother and his friend approached, I slowed to a walk to cool off. The sun was hot and there was no cloud cover.

"Keep running, Cole," my brother said.

"What?"

"Yeah, Cole. Keep running. You're not home yet," his friend said as they circled around behind me—almost close enough to skin the back of my legs with the black rubber of their tires. "Come on!"

"No. Stop it. I'm done," I said, just hoping they'd leave me alone.

"Go. Run. Come on. Run," they said getting closer. I started to pick up speed.

"Stop it!" I kept yelling, to no avail. I picked up the pace and kept running until I could take shelter in the garage of our house. My brother and his friend kept riding on down the block.

I would imagine this is a fairly normal kind of exchange between brothers. Older brother harasses younger brother. Younger brother feels helpless and angry. My guess is, if you have a brother (or even just a sibling) you've experienced something similar. And yet the biblical story of Joseph takes sibling rivalry to a whole new level. For me, being harassed by my brother and his friend meant running a little bit more. For Joseph, it meant suffering, pain, and a change to the entire course of his life.

You may have read the story of Joseph and know the basics. His father favored him, his brothers hated him. In fact, in a fit of rage, they tried to murder him. Having sympathy for Joseph, one of his brothers said, "No. Don't kill him. Let's sell him into slavery." The other brothers agreed, and they did so.

Joseph amazes me. From the beginning, his circumstances were so hard. He definitely could have laid down and said, "This sucks, God. I'm through with this. Here I am—away from my father, sold into slavery by my brothers, being treated like, well, a *slave*. I'm going to lay down and die." But he didn't. In fact, that's one of the things I most appreciate about Joseph. His circumstances didn't dictate his attitude, actions, or expectations. Rather, he understood his ability to change all those things by how he responded to them. His brothers meant it as an insult when they called him "this dreamer." But Joseph's ability to dream was actually what saved his life and the lives of all of Egypt and its surrounding nations.

Perhaps these dreams were able to save his life because they gave him a clear sense of his identity. Several stars in a circle bowing down to the star in the center. Sheaths of wheat, in a circle, bowing down the sheath of wheat in the center. For some reason, we often interpret these dreams as ego-centric. But they were prophetic. They gave him the ability to see something good about the future, rather than just something critical about the present. They were visions delivered from God, and despite the hell Joseph went through, he came out on the other side a blessing to his family and to many nations.

When the caravan of traders arrived in Egypt, Joseph was sold to Potiphar, one of Pharaoh's officials. And again, Joseph had a choice.

SPIRITUAL INNOVATION

He could lay down and die. He could live in a spirit of bitterness. He could try to run away. He could complain. He could get by on doing the bare minimum. But look at this.

When his master saw that the Lord was with him and that the Lord gave him success in everything he did, Joseph found favor in his eyes and became his attendant. Potiphar put him in charge of his household, and he entrusted to his care everything he owned. From the time he put him in charge of his household and of all that he owned, the Lord blessed the household of the Egyptian because of Joseph. The blessing of the Lord was on everything Potiphar had, both in the house and in the field. So he left in Joseph's care everything he had; with Joseph in charge, he did not concern himself with anything except the food he ate. (Genesis 39:3-6)

And when the Pharaoh needed a dream interpreted, Potiphar knew just the man for the job—Joseph. Because Joseph was a dreamer, he was a hard-worker, he saw things for what they could be, not necessarily for what they were. Joseph shifted things. And when God needs someone to shift things, He needs someone like Joseph.

BECOMING LIKE JOSEPH

In 2012, our church started looking for a building where we could meet. The process was not fun. You know why? Building owners don't want churches in their spaces. And I completely understand. Building owners who are trying to get people to come to the other spaces in their buildings often see the presence of a church in their space as an off-putting, uncreative, nail-in-the-coffin kind of move for their buildings.

Look around. It doesn't take much to find examples—on the street corners, on television—of the worst kinds of Christians. I'm not berating "the media." Their caricatures tend to be accurate and their perceptions are often based in reality. If I ran a television news program, I'd feature the kinds of Christians they're featuring, too. They're not fake. They're real people. They're just the ones who get a reaction and—in the end—increase viewership.

But the consequence is this: there are hundreds of thousands of people who walk the streets of downtowns, all across the country, every weekend, and the only foundation they have for understanding Christianity—and even worse, God—is the guy with the megaphone yelling at people from a distance

This is what our world thinks of Christianity, and sadly, it's affecting us more than we realize. It's affecting what non-Christians think about Christians and it's affecting what Christians think it means to be a Christian.

For example, let's take a look at the megaphone man. The easiest thing for any human to do is to say what we see. This is the first thing children learn to do when they learn to speak. They see objects and recognize them—ball, dog, baby. This is also the greatest tragedy of the megaphone man—he's lazy. He sees what is broken about the culture, the world, or individuals (or at least what he perceives to be broken), and stands at a distance, yelling about what he sees.

Is this what it means to be a Christian: to just notice and yell about what's broken around us?

Inherently, I think we know the "say what you see" approach is not helpful and yet, I experience this thing quite frequently. When I was in kindergarten, I got hit in the eye with a stick. It misshaped my pupil—the black spot in the middle of my iris. So my left eye kind of looks like a cat's eye. I've lived with this thing for over 20 years, and hundreds of times this has happened: Someone starts staring at my left eye and I notice it. They realize I've caught them staring, so they squint a little bit and cock their head. "Your eye..." they say, trailing off as they point or nod or make some sort of gesture or nervously

SPIRITUAL INNOVATION

blink. "Oh, I hope that's not offensive," they say more inquisitively than apologetically.

Honestly, I don't care. My vision is really poor in my left eye. I've lived with it so long it doesn't effect my daily life, and I've never been offended by someone asking about it or referencing it. But it's interesting. That phrase, "your eye... it's... different..." I know it's different. I've seen it before. I was there when it happened. You're not telling me anything new. There's no revelation there.

That's the story with the guy on the street corner. "Uh... your sin... it's... uh... sinful. I don't have anything else to say except... Uh... your sin... it's... uh... sinful... and I don't like you. I mean... I guess I could say that... yeah... I don't like you... That's why I have a megaphone... so we don't actually have to get close." Megaphones allow us to keep our distance, and as long as we can keep our distance, we'll never have to encounter the nuisance of relationship. We can just say what we see.

But when Joseph, who even lived before the cleansing sacrifice of Christ and the unleashing of the Holy Spirit, entered into Potiphar's house and Pharaoh's chambers, he didn't just say what he saw. He changed things, he shifted them. He dreamed and moved and was willing to see what was possible, as much as what was wrong. They were blown away by what Joseph did.

Joseph carried with him an atmosphere-shifting, culture-changing, life-giving authority. He did this because he was willing to do more than just say what he saw. He was willing to do the hard work it took to change it. The modern church has a lot to learn from Joseph in this sense. Too often, we have positioned ourselves in opposition to culture, standing at a distance, saying what we see, waiting for its demise. Too often, we miss what could be getting better, because we think things are only getting worse.

As Christians, what effect does the attitude of "things are getting worse" and "Jesus is coming back soon" have on the way we live our daily lives? More than you might think.

SELF-FULFILLING PROPHESY

When we have an expectation of doom, it colors the way we see the world. If we *believe* the world is getting worse, we'll set out to confirm what we believe.

Have you ever noticed this? When you believe something is true, your tendency will be to seek out pieces of information or evidence to reinforce that belief. To do this, we needn't look farther than the 24 hour news cycle or AM radio talk show hosts, hungry for anything "newsworthy." "Average" is not newsworthy. Most of the time, "good" is not newsworthy. Out-of-the-norm and bad is what our culture finds newsworthy. The result? We have entire channels on television that condense the worst events of the world and broadcast them with commentary into our living rooms 24 hours a day, 7 days a week. If your day is going well, just sit in front of a news station for half an hour and consume what they're serving. It'll paint a picture for you of what you've forgotten throughout your good day: The world is going to hell in a hand basket.

In the early years of my twenties, I consumed a lot of "news" and commentary. I would get in my car in the morning and turn on Glenn Beck. I would leave work for lunch and tune into Rush Limbaugh. I would get back to work and stream Sean Hannity over the Internet. And then, most of the day, Fox News would be playing in the background. Those days were some of the gloomiest days of my existence to date.

This is not a judgement of conservative politics, it's a statement that those shows are built upon finding ideologically dissonant ideas and exploiting them for increased listenership and to increase advertising revenue. Add this is what many conservative Christians are looking for—to reinforce their decided reality that the world is coming to an end. It's a dangerous combination. Suddenly you have an entire system that supports a worldview in which Barack Obama isn't only a liberal politician. He is a spiritual force ushering in the coming of the anti-Christ. It furthers the dissolution and sends us deeper down the spiral of defeatism.

There is evidence to support this observation about self-fulfilling prophecies. The medical community has done several studies, for example, showing how symptoms increase with symptom reporting. That is, the more a patient talks about his or her symptoms, the more the symptoms will appear. The tendency to have a negative view of the present and future makes the injury or illness itself a self-fulfilling prophecy. There's actually a psychological term for this confusion of reality. It's called "cognitive bias." Cognitive bias is the idea that sometimes we make judgements we don't realize we're making and those judgements are coloring the reality we experience.

Do you see what I'm getting at here? There is a danger lurking right in front of us: The more we believe the world is decaying, the more it will. The more we consume media from an industry who holds to the idea that "if it bleeds, it leads," the more we will report symptoms (although anecdotal) as the norm. The more we report these symptoms—or say what we see—the more we contribute to the increase of brokenness in the world.

I recently watched the 2009 documentary, "Transcendent Man." The documentary explores some components of the life and philosophies of inventor and futurist, Ray Kurzweil. In addition to his developments in music technology, Kurzweil has also been instrumental in the development of speech recognition software and artificial intelligence. His work in A.I. has led him to have some interesting hopes about humanity's future—many of which are easily susceptible to criticism. But it's not Kurzweil's viewpoints I want to discuss, rather an interesting observation of the documentary itself.

For 25 minutes, the documentary explores Kurzweil's work to leverage technology to fight disease and help the blind interface with the world. It isn't until 25 minutes into the film we hear the first dissenting opinion.

"It's going to be interesting to see if we can get through the next 10 or 20 years," the voice says, and when I look down and see the name of the organization, I realized: it's an organization whose name includes a greek word. "Of course!" I think. The first voice of doom we hear in the entire documentary is the voice of an evangelical. I google the organization, and on the front page are the phrases, "weathering the coming storm" and "anti-christ." I click on the "about" page and read, "we believe we are all heading into extremely turbulent times, which will test all our presumptions and beliefs." Not only that, part of their mission statement is, "to research, monitor and publish information to stimulate awareness of the strategic trends which impact our times and our personal ministries and stewardship." Inherent in their mission as an organization is to gather information that reinforces their belief that the world is getting worse, publish that information and anticipate that it will impact their ministry as well as the ministry of others.

Do you see the cycle here? It's the perpetuation of this mentality that becomes a self-fulfilling prophesy.

Throughout scripture, we see people of power with immense control of natural environments. There are people parting seas and rivers, making it rain or not rain, calming stormy weather, causing plants and bushes to wither or thrive. And here we are, positioned with all that precedent and—at best—we treat devastating weather phenomena as an inevitable reality for life on earth. At worst, we claim it as something God is unleashing on the earth in hopes of destroying humanity and teaching "those people" a lesson.

The result: a posture toward destruction that is either ambivalent or welcoming. A vengeful attitude towards people we don't know and toward whom we often have culturally induced animosity.

If the very people granted the keys to the kingdom of heaven have given up on bringing the revelation of that kingdom, who then will bring it?

The same is true with war. The most common American Evangelical posture towards war is one of welcoming. In the 2012 election, Mitt Romney's campaign included as part of his platform an increase in military spending by $2 trillion dollars, bringing US military spending to 4% of the country's GDP—the highest of any country in modern, civil society. "At the height of the British Empire, the British spending on defense was between 2 and 3 percent of national income," reports Thomas Ricks on foreignpolicy.com. In our fear and expectation of doom, we welcome war and—rather than praying for, advocating for, and setting an example of peace, American Evangelicals are one of the loudest leaders in war advocacy.

Is it any wonder we are so welcoming of war when we think the world is going to hell in a hand basket? After all, this world is meaningless. We pretty much need protection until Jesus comes back—right?

TO HELL IN A HANDBASKET

In addition to causing us to "give up" on the world we're currently living in and coloring the way we see events across the globe, the other problem with the "hell in a hand basket" and "Jesus is coming back soon" thinking is it prevents us from long term investment in spiritual stewardship. If the world is going to hell in a hand basket, it gives us permission to be in a perpetual state of defeat—a mindset that is in direct opposition with our true identity in Christ. And if Jesus is coming back next week, it gives us permission to be spiritually short-sighted. It allows us to think no farther than the scope and span of our own lives and miss out on the joys of setting a new spiritual standard for the coming generations.

Think about the widely-used metaphor of what happens when you make a copy of a copy. When you put an original in the copy machine, the machine takes a picture and it spits out a pretty high quality copy on the other side. But there are minor artifacts—dust particles, stray bits of ink, places where the ink didn't adhere—that have degraded the copy, just slightly. It's minor enough. This first copy is readable and probably looks only slightly different than the original. But then, you take this first copy, place it on top of the machine and make a copy of it. Then repeat. Eventually, several generations down the road, the document is unrecognizable.

The attempts of the Church to copy itself from one generation to the next have led us to a faith that is unrecognizable. The goal isn't to be one degraded copy after the other. The Church is meant to build upward from one generation to the next—to thrive, to exceed, to innovate.

The second law of thermodynamics states that, in an isolated system, things devolve toward entropy. In other words, if you roll a car along the ground, eventually the car will stop rolling. Am I the only one who feels like the church has isolated itself to the point where it has simply stopped moving, stopped rolling? We have surrendered but God is calling us to reclaim our power and purpose.

Under the law, we see a spiritual condition of God's manifested glory coming for a moment, then fading away. When Moses went up on the mountain, for example, met with God and was in his presence, he walked away radiating the glory of God from his countenance. Later, Moses covered his face because he didn't want the people to see the glory fading. I don't know about you, but I can identify with this. I'd rather have people see me at my best; I'd rather hide at my worst.

In 2 Corinthians, however, Paul paints a different picture for us living today in light of the cross and infilling of the Holy Spirit: he says, "But if the ministry of death, in letters engraved on stones, came with glory, so that the sons of Israel could not look intently at the face of Moses because of the glory of his face, fading as it was, how will the ministry of the Spirit fail to be even more with glory?" While there was a fleeting glory on the face of Moses, Paul tells us that "we all, with unveiled face, beholding as in a mirror the glory of the Lord, are being transformed into the same image, from glory to glory, just as from the Lord, the Spirit."

God has positioned us to move—not from much glory to less glory—but from some glory to more glory.

The good news is God's kingdom turns the laws of nature on their head. God has empowered and commissioned us to reverse the decaying effects of sin and thrust the world into a place of thriving.

TURN THE CORNER

It's time we change the way we think. It's time we change our expectations. It's time we live into the fullness of life with God.

Look at what Jesus said:

I will give you the keys of the kingdom of heaven; whatever you bind on earth will be bound in heaven, and whatever you loose on earth will be loosed in heaven. (Matthew 16:19)

Let me translate. If you think there's something broken about the world or your job or your boss or your neighborhood or your neighbor, and you're complaining about it... *stop it*! If you say you follow Jesus and yet you want to blame someone else for the problems around you... *stop it*!! If you're full of the Holy Spirit, and you claim to be a victim... *stop it*!!

This statement is two fold:

1. You have the keys to the kingdom of heaven.

That means the things stored up in heaven are yours to unleash. You and I are commissioned to pray, "Thy kingdom come, Thy will be done *on earth* as it is in heaven." And not only are we commissioned to pray those words, we are the conduits through whom God desires to unleash His unending, perfect, healthy, bountiful kingdom into the earth. This half of the statement is creative. You and I are co-laboring with God to unmask and deliver the kingdom of heaven.

2. Whatever you bind on earth will be bound in heaven.

This statement is a declaration of our power to wrangle up the broken parts of the world–sin, death, pain, hopelessness–and put them back into hell where they belong.

I was traveling from California back to Florida. That's a pretty long flight—one before which I typically spend time praying God will give me my own row or upgrade my ticket. Flying to and from Orlando means flying with lots of families. Kids are often irritable—because it's their first time on a plane or they're on their way to vacation and excited to arrive or have just finished a long week in the sun and ready to wind down. Regardless, some kids do great on planes, some do not.

Despite my best prayers to the contrary, my seat was not upgraded on this particular flight, and as our wheels left the ground in California, the toddler in the row in front of me began to cry. "Okay, I thought to myself. Not a big deal. Once we're in the air all will be okay." I was wrong. Hour one went by. Still crying. Hour two. Still crying. I honestly didn't know how she had so much stamina. If it wasn't so irritating, it would have been impressive. I was getting angsty. I could literally feel the tension building in the passengers in the surrounding rows as well. The older lady next to me kept taking deep breaths and letting them out of her nose. And she was breathing that tension right out into the airplane. I was picturing a cartoon bull with fire emanating from its nostrils as they shrank and grew with each inhale and exhale. The pit of my stomach was becoming more and more tense. And it seems babies are some of the most intuitive people on the planet.

As our tension increased, so did hers. And in a moment, I shifted. I shifted my thoughts and expectations and direction.

I prayed, "Lord, bring peace." I closed my eyes. I breathed in. "Lord, peace." I breathed out. I breathed that breath and that word of peace out into the airplane. And after hours of crying, in only a few minutes, the toddler was silent, sitting on the lap of her mother.

The tension and pain and discomfort—none of that was heavenly. I didn't want to experience it. The old lady next to me didn't want to experience it. The parents didn't want to be experiencing it. And the little girl absolutely didn't want to be experiencing it. It was an environment ripe for change. It was time to bind the pain and discomfort and unleash the peace of heaven into that cabin.

 A few minutes later, the little girl stood up. She looked over the back of the seat into the row where I was sitting. I saw her face for the first time. It was a light olive color. The redness I assume was there just moments ago had subsided. She looked at me, smiled and let out a cute little girl giggle. I smiled back. It was as if she knew I had something to do with the whole situation—like she felt a tangible peace flowing out of me and into her and the atmosphere around us.

What a simple, accurate example of Romans 8:18-21

I consider that our present sufferings are not worth comparing with the glory that will be revealed in us. The creation waits in eager expectation for the sons of God to be revealed. For the creation was subjected to frustration, not by its own choice, but by the will of the one who subjected it, in hope that the creation itself will be liberated from its bondage to decay and brought into the glorious freedom of the children of God.

This story was nothing more than a frustrated little girl on an airplane. What kind of hope and promise and opportunity do we see in famine and sickness and pain? Do we use them as evidence for the decay and destruction of the world or are we finally willing to step up and do something about them? I'm not talking about starting a non-profit or sending food or taking a mission trip to do some good things, although all those can be fine. I'm talking about living in true, spiritual, supernatural, problem-wrangling, heaven-unleashing, circumstance-shifting power.

As we discover who we are in Christ, the possibilities are endless. We no longer see ourselves as victims to our circumstances. We no longer see culture as doomed. Rather, we are filled with hope. When we are filled with hope, we are able to participate in manifesting the kingdom of heaven on earth.

QUESTIONS AND CONVERSATIONS :

- Are there things, people or places you've considered too far gone–unredeemable? How does God see those things or people? How can you see them in a new light?

SPIRITUAL INNOVATION

- In which areas of your life have you given up hope or considered yourself a victim to your circumstances? How can you shift your perception to understand the power and authority you have in those situations?

- Do you see yourself as a person who possesses supernatural power? Do you believe you have the ability to shift things? Why or why not?

DO SOMETHING :

Shift something. As you live life, keep your eyes open to the things, people and places around you. Walk into those situations understanding your ability to bring about redemption and restoration. Choose a specific moment this week to shift the atmosphere. Bring hope where there is hopelessness, love where there is hate, peace where there is unrest. Share your experience with someone.

SPIRITUAL INNOVATION // CHAPTER SIX
THE WORLD IS GETTING BETTER

SPIRITUAL INNOVATION

It was the first day of sixth grade. Math class. I walked into the portable classroom and chose a desk. There were a few kids I recognized from elementary school, but for the most part, all of us in the room were strangers to one another. We had all arrived a few minutes before the bell rang, making sure not to be late on the first day of school. It was less out of a desire to be prompt and more to avoid the potential awkwardness of walking in after class had started and becoming the center of attention. It seemed avoiding attention early on was the best way to leave room for identity formation in the coming weeks and months. Of course, our 12 year old minds didn't consciously think about these things, but everyone could sense in that room the tension between a desire for anonymity and the need to be accepted.

The bell rang and Ms. Workman got up to start talking. She was a gruff woman who never wore a dress. Work boots and green khakis were more her style. After a few minutes of introduction, the door swung open. In walked what seemed to be a 7-foot, broad-shouldered, hispanic girl. You would never have known this was her first day of sixth grade. I swear she had tattoos. She was exactly the person, I decided, in whose mind it was best to remain anonymous. "Alright. Find a seat," Ms. Workman said in her alto voice. The girl looked at Ms. Workman, flicked her head back, puckered her lips and made a clicking sound between her teeth and the fat of her cheeks.

The room was silent as the girl slowly walked—no, swaggered—past each row of desks, her sagging pants, high-top tennis shoes and long, black side ponytail swaying back and forth the whole way. We each separately breathed a sigh of relief as she passed by. When she came to the row next to mine, however, she turned to walk up it. I didn't want to stare directly into her eyes (this was a sign of challenge, I figured) yet I didn't want to seem weak by avoiding eye contact altogether. So when she walked up to the row and sat right next to me, I looked over, gave a slight smile and looked away.

Over the coming weeks, the tension lessened. I found out her name was Crystal. Only now do I realize the irony in the contrast of her personality and name. Some days, Crystal would be playful. Other days, I swear she was running off the adrenaline I can only imagine came from a Spanish mafia hit job. I was well aware that no matter how friendly we became, at any moment, she could and would squash me into the floor. Crystal never had a reason to get into it with me, but I did see her fury unleashed on more than one occasion. She was definitely a textbook bully and bullying seemed to be an accepted part of what it meant to grow up in an American Middle School.

A couple years ago, I saw my first "anti-bullying" campaign ad. The concept was foreign to me. In fact, I think I had some aversion to it. "Oh come on. Just let it go. It's a part of growing up," I thought to myself. Bullying seemed to be so engrained in our culture, it was foreign to even think of it as a bad thing worth eliminating. But it is. Not only that, it's an amazing example of the growth of our culture—a culture in which violence is on the decline.

A WORLD AT PEACE

Steven Pinker, Harvard professor of cognitive psychology and author of "The Better Angels of our Nature: Why Violence Has Declined," says "today, we're probably living in the most peaceful time in our species existence." Looking at images of the holocaust, experiencing events like September 11, 2001, the attack at the Boston Marathon in 2013 and watching and listening to the 24 hour news cycle make this hard to believe. Our romanticized collective understanding of the past paints it in a light of peace, harmony and upright morality, but that just isn't the case.

Pinker, in his 2007 TED talk further explains his statement. Until 10,000 years ago, humans lived in hunter/gatherer groups. The best evidence we have for the peaceful or violent nature of these societies is by gathering data of modern hunter/gatherer groups alive today. In his research of modern hunter/gatherer societies in the New Guinea Highlands and the Amazon Rain Forest, University of Chicago professor Lawrence Keeley, reports the percentage of male deaths due to warfare linger between near 60 percent in some groups and 15 percent in others. To keep up with this rate, violent deaths in the US and Europe in the twentieth century would have to have been close to 2 billion, according to Pinker. Instead, it was about 100 million—including both world wars.

Jared Diamond, in his book "The World Until Yesterday" talks about what would happen if two people from these different nomadic tribes met one another. In an April 2013 *This American Life* Episode, Diamond describes it this way: "If you ran across a strange person on your land, that could only mean they were there for some bad reason. They were there to scout out your land for a raid or to steal a woman or to steal a pig, and so if you ran into a strange person in the forest, and you couldn't run away from him—you came around a corner and there he was—then the two of you would sit down and have a long conversation in which each of you named all your relatives trying to find some relative in common which gives you a reason not to kill each other. And, if after two hours you haven't found any relative in common, then one of you starts running or you try to kill the other person."

And things haven't just gotten better between "tribes." The way we treat those inside our own tribes has changed as well.

Throughout history, we know mutilation and torture were accepted practices and punishments in cultures the world over. People's tongues were cut out, ears were cut off and eyes were cut out or burned. These were not uncommon punishments for infractions like stealing. Corporal punishment included being burned alive, drowned, torn apart on a large wheel or by horses pulling in opposite directions and the death penalty was issued for non-violent crimes such as speaking ill of the king or stealing a loaf of bread. Slavery was a common and accepted practice and cruelty was a common form of entertainment.

The estimated rate of homicides during the middle ages was 100 per 100,000 people per year. The rate went down to less than 1 per 100,000 in 7 or 8 European countries with a slight up curve around the 1960s. And since the 1990s, those rates have lowered again.

Since 1945, there has been a steep decline in interstate wars, deadly ethnic riots and military coups in Europe and the Americas. Worldwide, there has been a steep decline in deaths from interstate wars. In the 1950s, the average death per conflict per year was over 65,000. Today, there are less than 2,000 deaths per conflict per year.

There has been a 90% reduction in genocides since World War II.

So, as Pinker puts it, "why are so many people so wrong about something so important?" Pinker gives a few reasons he believes this to be the case. Among others,

1. Better reporting: I'll remove Pinker's value word "better" and describe it as we have already—24 hour delivery of bad news as it happens from around the globe.

2. Cognitive illusion: The fact that we are more prone to remember gory images and stories from the news than good ones.

3. Opinion and Advocacy Markets: In order to raise funds for causes, it is necessary for advocacy groups to paint a certain picture. As Pinker puts it, "No one ever attracted observers, advocates and donors by saying, 'things just seem to keep getting better and better.'"

4. Change in standards outpaces change in behavior: Our standards for acceptable and unacceptable behavior change. Often that standard is ahead of the present reality. This is what we're seeing with anti-bullying campaigns. When our nation was focused on ending a world war, bullying wasn't paid much attention. But in times of greater peace, we're able to notice and eradicate other, less severe forms of violence.

A while back, I watched several episodes of the HBO series, *Deadwood*. The show depicts life as it was in the gold rush town of Deadwood, South Dakota in the 1870s. Creator David Milch did thorough historical research before the series was produced and strived for accuracy. Thus, the show is full of the open acceptance of nudity and prostitution, gratuitous profanity (although there is dispute over the authenticity of the specific words used), murder, usury, the mistreatment of women and rampant racism. It's a far cry from the sterilized west of the John Wayne films. Most of what was common in daily life in the era depicted in the show is starkly different than what is acceptable in 21st century America. It's a small window (although one I do not recommend opening) into how society and culture have shifted in only 150 years.

We might look at the news today and be appalled by a shooting at a mall or public place (and we should be), but chances are we would be more appalled by the lack of established laws and vigilantly justice amongst the residents of the mining camps of the American west. The accused often didn't have legal representation and the punishments would often not fit the crime. Lawlessness abounded, and "victimless crimes" often went unpunished. (Gordon Morris Bakken (2000). Law in the western United States, University of Oklahoma Press. pp. 209-14.)

We see this cultural shift happening, even now. In a National Geographic interview, former Aryan Brotherhood Enforcer, Casper Crowell acknowledged that "Many things I myself have done, I would have been knighted for a thousand years ago. I would have been, at the very least, labeled a hero—a good citizen. But the laws of today have made me an outlaw, a killer, a monster." (National Geographic, Aryan Brotherhood Documentary, March 4, 2007)

Fortunately, our society is increasingly averse to violence, and as we see a decrease in the most violent crimes, like genocide and homicide, we become more acutely aware of the less blatant, less obvious forms of violence and are working to eradicate them as well.

FREEDOM, HEALTH AND POVERTY

It's not only a lessening of violent deaths that has occurred throughout human history. It's also a drastic change in the quality of life. The evolution of the role of women in society is a great example. For millennia, women were treated as nothing more than property. In his story above, notice Jared Diamond said raiding parties on another tribes' land would be there "to steal a woman or to steal a pig." Women and livestock were viewed in much the same way for a great deal of history—as a commodity used for a utilitarian purpose. Even as society progressed, women were forced to remain silent and uneducated. In the US, women weren't given the right to vote until 1920. But in recent decades, we've seen a sharp upturn in the opportunities and rights of women worldwide.

In the 1970s, women passed men in college enrollment in the United States, and the trend continues today.

Even in countries where women are still subjected to slavery and prostitution, we're seeing incredible work of global organizations working to free women and provide necessary education and resources for their liberation.

Over the last 40 years, we have seen a drastic increase in the litera-

SPIRITUAL INNOVATION

cy of women in countries all over the world. In many middle-eastern countries, the literacy rate has gone from the 20%-30% mark to the 80%-100% mark in just the last four decades.

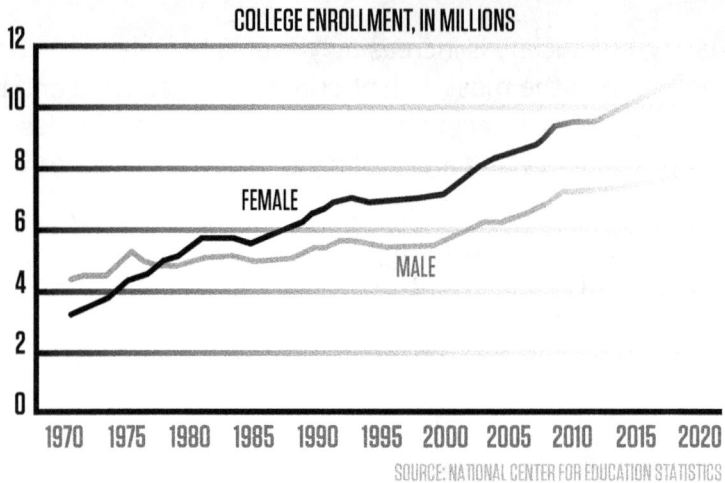

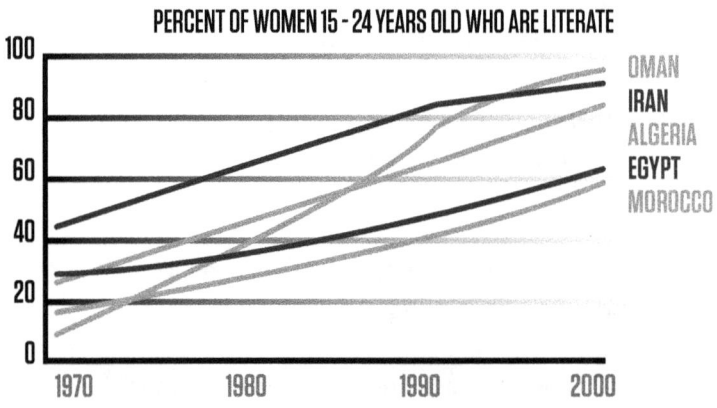

(United Nations Educational, Scientific and Cultural Organization (UNESCO) Institute for Statistics, "Literacy Statistics" (www.uis.unesco.org, accessed March 11, 2003))

We see a similar story with slavery. Something that was once an acceptable part of western society is now being eliminated from the face of the planet. Kevin Bales is the co-founder of Free the Slaves, whose mission it is to end all forms of human slavery within the next 25 years. In his 2010 TED talk, he paints a hopeful picture.

The 27 million people who are in slavery today—that's a lot of people. But it's also the smallest fraction of the global population to ever be in slavery. And likewise, the 40 billion dollars that they generate into the global economy each year is the tiniest proportion of the global economy to ever be represented by slave labor.

Slavery, illegal in every country, has been pushed to the edges of our global society. And in a way, without us even noticing, has ended up standing on the precipice of its own extinction, waiting for us to give it a big boot and knock it over. And get rid of it. And it can be done.

Just for perspective, today there are 3.9 slaves for every 1,000 people in the world. The 1860 US census, on the other hand, reported that 393,975 individuals owned 3,950,528 slaves. (http://www.civil-war.net/pages/1860_census.html). That means 125 slaves were owned per 1000 people in the US. Neither number is acceptable, but in the last 150 years, we have come so far in eliminating the plague of slavery.

In the same way we see organizations around the globe working to eradicate the mistreatment of women, we see new leaders and non-profits everyday working to eradicate slavery. These initiatives are not built on pipe dreams. These organizations are working diligently with the expectation that their efforts will eradicate these issue altogether.

Next comes the conversation on global poverty—also moving in a positive direction. Let's look at yet another TED talk, this one by American engineer and entrepreneur, Peter Diamandis. Diamandis

SPIRITUAL INNOVATION

is also the founder of the X Prize Foundation, "an educational non-profit organization whose mission is to bring about radical breakthroughs for the benefit of humanity." In his talk, titled "Abundance Is Our Future," Diamandis presents some hopeful statistics on global poverty.

In the last 100 years:

Per capita income is up 3 times.
The cost of food has fallen 10 times.
The cost of electricity is down 20 times.
The cost of transportation is down 100 times.
The cost of communication is down 1000 times.

Of the Americans under the poverty line today:

99% have electricity, running water, a toilet, and a refrigerator.
95% have a television.
88% have a mobile telephone.
70% have a car and air conditioning.

Diamandis notes that today, a majority of Americans in poverty have immediate access through mobile technology to more information than President Reagan had during his terms in office in the 1980s.

In addition to the lessening of poverty and its changing definition, we've seen significant shifts in global health. In the last 100 years, humans are living twice as long and childhood mortality is down 10 times.

"But haven't you seen the atrocities in third world countries?!" I'm often asked. The answer is, "yes." I've seen poverty in countries around the world. I've met people who don't have enough to eat and live in squalor. There is absolutely more to be done. But the beautiful thing is there is less poverty, sickness, and violence today than ever before and there's more being done to eradicate all three than humanity has ever seen.

It's not coincidence that I've cited so many TED talks in this chapter of the book. TED is dedicated to providing a platform for sharing "ideas worth spreading." They seek out people who are experts in their field, committed to solving the world's problems. These are people who see a problem in the world—just like megaphone man—but rather than let it go because after all, "the world is going to hell in a hand basket," these are the people who believe the problem is solvable. Not only is the problem solvable, they see their ability to put their hands, hearts, minds and spirits to work to see it solved.

The work of TED is an example of the power of believing the world can get better and actually seeing it come to fruition.

These men and women working to end earth's atrocities are like the ones running into burning buildings or carrying the wounded after a terrorist attack. There are some in the Church running alongside them in the work—even at times, leading in their own rite. Other times, the Church is like those standing around, stunned and immobilized on the street outside. At times we're even like the terrorists themselves, cheering at the evil in the world, seeing it as a means to our anticipated end.

Often, when I talk about the world getting better, Christians respond with pushback—not because their experience suggests otherwise, but because their theological standpoint necessitates it. That's what amazes me. When you think of your family and your children and friends, when you consider the people you work alongside of and come into contact with as you go about your life, chances are, your assessment of the world is pretty great. The food you get to eat, the amenities surrounding you, your house, your car, your technology, your stuff—looking at the state of these things, you're most likely to say things are a-okay.

SPIRITUAL INNOVATION

It's not our lives or experiences that lead us to view the world as destined for destruction. No. It's our modern Evangelical machine—complete with an Apocalyptic industry of movies, books, t-shirts, and doormats. It has led us to give up on the world and anticipate its demise. But the truth is, the world is increasingly becoming a more peaceful, healthy place to live—and live longer.

The Church has a choice. We can either be the voice believing and calling for things to get worse; *or* we can be the voice believing things are already getting better and we can summon our communities to wake up to our calling and lead them that way. Because even if physical poverty and hunger is eradicated, the spirit of humanity is still looking for spiritual satisfaction. If we see the end of war, we still need inner peace. If human slavery comes to an end, there is still a great need for freedom from the bondage of spiritual oppression.

A world in which humanity is freed from the search for day-to-day physical sustenance is a world ripe for Spiritual Innovation. Because if the world truly is getting better, if the kingdom is really to come as Christ prayed, the Church better be poised for the future. Not a future of destruction. Rather, a future that sees a continual increase in the revelation of the infinite character and nature of God on the earth.

QUESTIONS AND CONVERSATIONS :

- What factors do you use to assess your view of the world around you? How do those things affect your outlook on the world?

- What are some things you're celebrating about your life or the lives of those around you right now? What does the overall state of your life say about the state of the world?

- What are some improvements you've seen in the world during the span of your lifetime? What do those things say about the state of the world?

DO SOMETHING :

Inject good news. At some point in the next few days, you will find yourself in a conversation (or contributing to a conversation) that is full of complaining. Notice it. Recognize it. Help the conversation take a step back and see the bigger picture. Move the conversation from complaint to celebration.

SPIRITUAL INNOVATION // CHAPTER SEVEN
EXPLORE THE POSSIBILITIES

If this is all true—that the world is getting better, that God is bringing His hope and redemption to the earth right now as we're living in it, that we don't have to hold on and wait until Jesus comes back—it changes the way we live out our faith, right? We can't simply mimic the spiritual practices of those who have come before us or copy what is happening all around us. We have to innovate a new way to relate to God. God may want to do something here and now through you that He has never done before. Look around you. Consider your life. Now, recognize this statement is true for you. "God wants to do something in this time, in this place, to uniquely reveal Himself through me."

Something supernatural is already happening. There is a new breed of dreamers living on the face of the earth today. Stories of biblical proportions are coming from the Muslim world. Ali—a Muslim man who was on a hajj to Mecca—is one of those stories. On the first night of his spiritual journey, something quite unexpected happened.

"That night I saw Jesus in a dream," he recalls. "First, Jesus touched my forehead with his finger. And after touching me, He said, 'You belong to me,'"

That encounter with Jesus in a dream changed the direction of Ali's life. His story is told in a documentary called *More Than Dreams*. And Ali's story doesn't stand alone.

"We're seeing that all around. We're hearing about people that have never even thought about Jesus as savior," Tom Doyle, with e3 Ministries, said. "They're content Muslims and they're having dreams over and over." (http://www.charismanews.com/world/33713-dreams-visions-moving-muslims-to-christ)

These stories are reminiscent of the Apostle Paul's encounter with Jesus on the road to Damascus and they are on the rise—testimonies of people having clear, direct encounters with Jesus. Jesus speaks to them and their lives are forever changed.

In this chapter, I want us to explore the power and authority of God's voice alive and well in our modern age. What do His words mean for us? And what do we do when God speaks?

Let's bring this idea a little closer to home with a fictitious story—in which you are the main character.

Say one day you are spending time with God—however that looks for you–and in this time, you take out a pen and a piece of paper and begin writing. You write three or four sentences. A little confused as to their meaning, you read them over a few times, fold up the paper and put it in your pocket.

Now for the sake of this story, let's say you wrote this while living in the mountains of Appalachia. You've actually never been in contact with the outside world. You've never read the Bible before, nor have you heard anyone quote it. The only people you know are your aging mother and father, your brother—Jed or Cletus, you pick—and your sister, Molly Anne. That afternoon, there's a knock on the door. "What's that?" you think to yourself. Being isolated, the concept of knocking on the front door of the house isn't something you've ever considered. Sure, your family knocks on the door of your bedroom when they need you, but why would anyone ever knock on the front door?

"Molly Anne?" you yell. Then, from the other side of the door, the voice of a man you've never heard before says, "ummm, no. My name is Samuel McKinlay." It's a timid voice, a bit shaky. You're intrigued.

"Well, what do you want?" you ask, followed by a quick, "Come in here." You're excited and not quite as timid as the man on the other side of the door. The door swings open, and the man is a slight silhouette in the light of the sun, pouring into the unlit room. The only other light is spilling in from a window in the wall behind you. It casts a cool, white-ish light on the simple, mostly wooden objects in the room.

"Well, what is it?" you ask.

"Hi sir. I'm Samuel McKinlay. I'm from the town at the foot of the mountain. I've come to give you this Bible."

You've heard of the Bible from your parents. They've referenced some stories, but it's nothing you've ever read before.

"Alright, give it here then," you say, leaning forward in the chair and holding out your hand. The man slowly walks through the threshold of the doorway and into the room and places the Bible in your outstretched hand. You grasp the book and flip through the pages. "Okay. That'll be all. Get along now."

The man takes a deep breath. "Okay, sir. I was wondering, if I could… perhaps I could come back in a few days and talk a bit."

"Whatever suits you."

With that, the man backs away and out the door. It shuts behind him and you're left to rifle through the pages somewhat aimlessly. That's when it happens: you land somewhere toward the end and begin reading. There, you recognize two of the sentences. "To him who overcomes, I will give some of the hidden manna. I will also give him a white stone with a new name written on it, known only to him who receives it." You stand up. The book falls to the floor as you reach your hand into your pocket and pull out the now-crumpled paper from that morning. You pick the Bible up and turn back to the passage as you walk to the table. Placing the crumpled paper on the table next to the Bible, you compare the scrawled words to the printed text in this passage. They are identical!

"What does it mean?!" you ask yourself, startled.

THE WORDS

So that's the story. Now I have a question. Lean in close. I have to whisper this because I'm not sure if I'm allowed to actually ask it. Were you, in the moment you wrote those sentences, any less inspired than John when he recorded those words in the book of Revelation? Okay, come in a little closer. I have another question—one I *know* is off limits, one many people might find too dangerous to even ask. What about the sentences you wrote just before and after this matching passage? Could they be inspired, too?

I know the details of this story aren't true. It's a hypothetical anecdote, and we could tell those kinds of stories all day long. But chances are, if you're listening, you've had moments of divine revelation. Have you ever had someone say something to you that you knew was from God? Has someone ever said something that made the spirit inside you jump, something that resonated so deeply you just knew it was divine?

What about the story of Ali and the dozens of stories like his coming out the Middle East? Is there a difference between the revelation of Jesus to these Muslims today and what happened to Paul as he was traveling to Damascus? Don't the stories sound the same? Is it possible God's voice is loud and clear and He still has things to say to us here and now?

In the process of writing this book, there were several moments in which the process just seemed too hard to keep going. I was wrestling with the insecurity of how people might respond to these ideas and, ultimately, to me. There were moments I decided, "Eh, I think I'll just stop." It was in the middle of one of these moments that I went to my friends', Sam and Kristen's, house. They had gathered some people to speak life and encouragement over one another and that sounded good to me. The process was simple. We would sit, listen and write what we heard. After a time, we'd speak what we had written for each of the people in the room. It was a free environment. Sam set it up wisely saying, "We'll say some things here—it's your job to go away and bring them before God to discern them."

I didn't know most of the people in their living room that night, and they didn't know me. But when it came time to speak what they had heard for me, the first person spoke, "Don't quit. What God wants to say through you is important. You need to keep going." There was a resounding "woah" in the room as four or five other people turned their papers around to reveal an almost identical message.

In the same way God has spoken to me through others, He's sometime spoken to me for others.

It has taken awhile to develop a sense of understanding when it's Him, but over time, as I've been expectant of His voice speaking to me and through me, I've come to have a better understanding of when it's God and when it's me. Just as there's a perceptible difference between saying something that's a good thought from the mind of Cole and something that's spoken from my emotions, there's also a perceptible difference between when I'm speaking from my mind or emotions and when something has been implanted by the Spirit. It comes from a different place. For me, it feels like it wells up from the gut and informs my mind and emotions. It feels as if God has placed a seed in me and it grows outward and upward—the fruit of it bearing in my mind and heart.

It happens in the strangest of places—but that seems to be the way God works. Once, I was sitting in a sports bar with some friends. We were there to have a creative meeting for some work we were doing together. There were eight or so of us, and as one of the guys was speaking, I felt one of those seeds drop in and grow. I didn't say anything right then, but later, I took my friend aside and told him what I had heard about what God was saying for him in his new role and in the new season of his life. There was no bolt of lighting. He didn't break down crying. He received it, he held it closely and he took it away to bring it before God in his own time with Him.

Have you ever heard God speak? Has He ever spoken to you or through you? What did you make of it?

The reason I think these questions are important is because how we view these moments dictates what we do with what we hear. We often have a "take it or leave it" attitude toward moments like these. They slip away unremembered. They are viewed as lesser words of God and aren't taken seriously. But if we're to move into a place of developing intimacy with and relationship to God, if we're going to be spiritually innovative, if we want to engage with the way God is working in the world right here and right now, we must be people who are not only willing to expect these moments but to take them seriously—to write them down, to impress them upon our hearts, and to carry them with us.

THE CONSTANT THREAD

In our modern, western context, we often say that God is the same yesterday, today and forever. We believe we have the same Holy Spirit in us as Paul and Peter and the rest of the apostles and believers in the New Testament Church. But we usually expect so much less. In fact, there are many who might find the questions I asked above sacrilegious or dangerous. Perhaps you find yourself wondering, as you read, if these questions should even be considered.

That uneasy feeling stems from the modern fight to champion the

Bible as the "authoritative word of God." And in this chapter, my agenda is not to lessen the power of God's voice revealed to us through what is written in the Bible. No. It's to champion the consistent power of the presence and voice of an active God, living with us today in the form of the Holy Spirit. That's the constant thread.

We can't, in good conscience, be believers in Christ without considering God's activity among us—right now, today. And yet, this is such a hard pill to swallow for the modern church because we've placed the words and events of the Bible on such a pedestal, we can't even imagine how what's happening in our midst could possibly compare. I think this is a grave mistake. Simply put, one of the greatest mistakes of the modern Church is we believe (or at least act like we believe) an infinite God has already revealed everything He wants us to know.

Is that even a proper stance?

At the end of the book of Revelation, John writes, "I warn everyone who hears the words of the prophecy of this book: if anyone adds anything to them, God will add to him the plagues described in this book."

Historically we have applied this statement to the Bible. There it is, conveniently at the end of the entire book, like a declaration: "The things God says here—in the collected works of the Bible—are the only words He'll ever say with gravity and authority. All other words, written or spoken, from this moment forward, will be of less spiritual significance or inspiration. Therefore, no other words should ever be considered to be equally inspired as the words written here."

But before we commit to that ideology, let's think about when John wrote his revelation down. It was not in the context of the other works of the Bible. The "Bible," as we know it, didn't even exist at that time. In fact, there was not even a consideration in his mind that his words would be included in a compilation of other writings considered to be "holy." John experienced a revelation and recorded it as a testimony of that revelation. It was certainly meant to be read. But John didn't even anticipate the world would continue to exist for the subsequent 2,000 years, much less that we would be reading his work in a collection of holy writings.

As we answer the questions above (is the Bible the end of God's revelation to humanity?), let's first take a look at the canonization of the Bible—how, when and why it was compiled.

The first versions of the New Testament appeared around 400 AD. With the existing Old Testament books, they totaled 73 in all, a number that remained the same for the subsequent 1100 years. That's when Martin Luther arrived on the scene and moved seven of the books from the Old Testament to a middle section between the Old and New Testaments in 1534. He include the disclaimer that, "these books are not held equal to the scriptures but are useful and good to read." Additionally, Luther rearranged the New Testament, including the books of Hebrews and James at the end, along with Jude and Revelation, because he considered them to be less reputable. Even the 1611 King James Bible included the additional books between the Old and New Testaments. Today, the Catholic and Orthodox bibles include the original 73 books, while the modern Protestant Bible includes only 66.

These facts are not included here to raise questions as to the veracity of the Bible. They are included here to help us realize that the questions we're asking above are as old as recorded human history. People, until the last few hundred years, have been asking, "What is God saying?" And yet for those of us who have grown up steeped in the rhetoric about the inerrancy of Scripture, we've neglected to ask the question altogether. We have assumed that, whatever God might want to say has already been said to someone else, in a time prior to ours. To me, this is the greatest tragedy.

SPIRITUAL INNOVATION

At the beginning of the protestant reformation, there was formulated an idea known today as the Five Solae: Sola scriptura (by scripture alone), Sola fide (by faith alone), Sola gratia (by grace alone), Solus Christus (through Christ alone), Soli Deo gloria (glory to God alone). There are some great concepts in here, but let's take a look at that first statement—Sola scriptura.

One of the intentions behind the statement was to question the Magisterium, or the belief that only leaders in the The Church had the the ability to rightly and properly interpret scripture. This was a helpful step in recognizing the priesthood of all believers and empowering individuals to thrive in their intimate, personal relationship with God. However, this has not been the most predominant effect of Sola Scriptura on modern Christian culture. The primary effect has been that an attitude of exclusivity and sanctity of the scriptures has been accepted and elevated by Protestantism, without question. In other words, we have been conditioned to believe the Bible is the only inspired, authoritative word of God. Within Protestantism, this idea is held to be so unquestionably true, it would be considered sacrilegious to question it's veracity.

Yet, the questions must be asked: Is the Bible the only and final word of God? Is God finished speaking?

First, let's ask this question, "When the reformists said 'Sola scriptura,' did they perceive the scriptures to be the same thing we do?" Based on the information I related earlier in this chapter—the discrepancy of 73 books vs our current 66, knowing Luther's objections to the books of Hebrews, James , Jude and Revelation—the answer is "no." The reformers had a largely similar, yet slightly different, perception of what the scriptures actually were.

Next, I would ask, "Would the New Testament writers themselves agree with and adhere to Sola Scriptura?" I have to say, I don't think so. It might make you cringe to hear me say that, but the biggest problem is this: Had the New Testament writers believed in Sola Scriptura, we wouldn't have a Bible at all. We would only have Old Testament writings grouped together as a holy book. We wouldn't have added or subtracted anything when Jesus came, or when the early church was growing. The writings of Paul and the gospels would be books on the shelf along with Ignatius, Tozer, Saint Augustine and anyone else who's written since the time of Christ.

And this brings me to the biggest dilemma of Sola Scriptura. It, in itself, is extra-biblical. It breaks its own rule. There's no scripture that says, "God has stopped communicating to people with clarity and authority." On the contrary. Every time God speaks, He speaks with authority. The New Testament reality is one of God speaking *to* and *through* individuals on a regular basis. The New Testament reality is one that includes language, examples, and instruction around the ongoing revelation of God's voice through His people.

So where did we get the idea He was done speaking? And what would happen if we began to listen for His sovereign voice in our lives today? If you ask me, it would look a little bit like Spiritual Innovation.

THE SPIRIT OF WISDOM AND REVELATION

We have, in our culture, the word apocalypse, meaning some cataclysmic event perpetuating the end of the world. The word is actually derived from the original Greek word for Revelation as used in the beginning of John's book. This Greek word, apocalypses, has quite a different meaning than our modern "apocalypse." Here are the definitions:

APOCALYPSES
1) laying bare, making naked
2) a disclosure of truth, instruction

> a) *concerning things before unknown*
> b) *used of events by which things or states or persons hitherto withdrawn from view are made visible to all*
>
> 3) *manifestation, appearance*

This word, Revelation, was not used to represent a disastrous event, but rather to denote the spiritual derivation of a vision. It wasn't simply an opinion. It wasn't something John learned by hearing or reading. It wasn't only a good idea. It was something different—a revelation. An apocalypses. It was like that moment I had when God spoke to me about my friend in the sports bar.

In Matthew 16, Jesus asks his disciples, "Who do you say I am?" Simon Peter answers, "You are the Messiah, the Son of the living God." And in verse 17, Jesus uses the verb form, apokalypt, in saying, "Blessed are you, Simon son of Jonah, for this was not *revealed* to you by flesh and blood, but by my Father in heaven." Peter's revelation was a divinely inspired word, confirming the divine nature of Jesus. It is upon this *revelation* that all of the Church is built. And, like Peter, we have the opportunity to listen intimately to the Holy Spirit as He continues to reveal the nature and work of Jesus.

Apocalypses is used several other times throughout the New Testament, acting as small reminders that we should live in a posture of expectation for ongoing spiritual revelation. God was and *is* speaking, to and through the Church. We should not only be expecting the revelation of the saving message of Christ, but also a revelation about what we should do, how we should act, where we should go, what words we should use and how to find healing and redemption. If we listen, we will find God's voice, presence and kingdom throughout the universe.

Paul's firsthand experience with such revelation is recorded in several of his letters to the churches. In Ephesians 3:2-6, Paul gives one such account.

Surely you have heard about the administration of God's grace that was given to me for you, that is, the mystery made known to me by **REVELATION***, as I have already written briefly. In reading this, then, you will be able to understand my insight into the mystery of Christ, which was not made known to men in other generations as it has now been revealed by the Spirit to God's holy apostles and prophets. This mystery is that through the gospel the Gentiles are heirs together with Israel, members together of one body, and sharers together in the promise in Christ Jesus.*

The very message of the salvation of the gentiles, through the sacrifice and resurrection of Christ on the cross, was not derived from something Paul was taught or something he read or conceived intellectually as the result of reading the Old Testament scriptures. Paul here, states that he has come to understand the mystery of Christ revealed to the Gentiles as the result of spiritual revelation. That is, he has received a direct message from God. The message had heretofore been hidden but then was made known to Paul as the result of a divine directive. As a result, Paul brought the message of salvation and the infilling of the Holy Spirit to the Gentiles, so they would become co-heirs and sharers of the promise of Christ Jesus.

Can you imagine how things might have gone differently if Paul would have said to himself, "This can't be true because it's not in the Old Testament," or "Who am I to receive the revelation of Christ?" or "God doesn't speak anymore".

We see another account of Paul receiving revelation in 2 Corinthians 12:1-4.

I must go on boasting. Although there is nothing to be gained, I will go on to visions and **REVELATIONS** *from the Lord. I know a man in Christ who fourteen years ago was caught up to the third heaven. Whether it was in the body or out of the body I do not know—God knows. And I know that this man—whether in the body or apart from the body I do not know, but God knows—was caught up to paradise. He heard inexpressible things,*

things that man is not permitted to tell.

Many biblical scholars believe Paul is, indeed, testifying to a personal experience. In this experience, he received a personal revelation, something not to be shared with others. It was an intimate encounter with God in which Paul received a specific revelation meant to be kept private—at least at that time. But we do see Paul affirming spiritual revelation, not only through the apostles, but through the Church as a whole, in two passages. In Ephesians 1:17-19, Paul recounts his prayers for the church in Ephesus.

I keep asking that the God of our Lord Jesus Christ, the glorious Father, may give you the Spirit of wisdom and **REVELATION***, so that you may know him better. I pray also that the eyes of your heart may be enlightened in order that you may know the hope to which he has called you, the riches of his glorious inheritance in the saints, and his incomparably great power for us who believe.*

In this passage, Paul prays that the Church in Ephesus would be granted the spirit of revelation. He prays the believers in Ephesus would have the same types of divine revelation John would later have as recorded in his book of Revelation. Additionally, Paul includes revelation in his instructions to the Corinthian Church on propriety in worship.

What then shall we say, brothers? When you come together, everyone has a hymn, or a word of instruction, a **REVELATION***, a tongue or an interpretation. All of these must be done for the strengthening of the church. (1 Corinthians 14:26)*

Here, Paul makes a distinct differentiation between each of these verbal offerings in the context of worship. A hymn is different from a word of instruction which is different from a tongue or an interpretation which is different from revelation. Paul includes apocalypses here as a unique contribution for the strengthening of the Church.

In the early church, these kinds of revelations weren't just accepted, they were expected. Individuals of the community would consistently hear from and communicate on behalf of God by means of spiritual revelation. This revelation was distinctly different from each of the other things listed in this passage and had its own unique origin and purpose.

In the same way we still sing songs and give instruction and speak in tongues and have translation, we are also to make ourselves available to the revelation of the Holy Spirit for the strengthening of our personal relationship with God, as well as for the Church. We must move beyond the belief that everything to be known about God has already been made known. We must reawaken to the reality that an infinite God still desires to reveal His manifold wisdom through the Church. God is limitless and desires to reveal the nature of His character and his plans for you and me and the world—both *to* and *through* us.

THE NECESSARY UNEASINESS OF REVELATION

My friend Carlos talks about the mission of his life as being someone who disturbs and disrupts the career Christian. He sees value in this because, from his perspective, religion grows best in an atmosphere of comfort and control, while faith grows best in an atmosphere of questioning and openness to new ideas.

When it comes to the topic of revelation we're discussing in this chapter, I see how it can both disturb and disrupt the career Christian. The idea that God is still speaking with power and authority isn't hard for us to wrap our minds around because it's contrary to what we believe. It's hard for us to wrap our minds around because, if we walk down that road, it will disturb and disrupt the structures of control and order we've applied to our lives. This is not a crisis of belief. It's a crisis of life. How does the idea of God speaking to us disturb our lives?

1. IT GIVES US POWER.

If God is saying things to us and through us, it takes the power we have in our lives to an entirely new level. We can no longer be content to simply exist in the social club of the American Evangelical Church. We are commissioned into a life of listening and responding, a life of acting without precedent. That kind of authority and power makes us uncomfortable.

2. IT GIVES US RESPONSIBILITY.

As every superhero knows, with great power comes great responsibility. Let's be honest. Living a life steeped in entertainment and distraction can be a comfortable life. But that's not what we're created for. We're created for something much larger and that thing thrives in direct correlation to our stewardship of it.

3. IT MAKES US WORK.

Knowing you have power and ability to alter your life and surroundings instills an underlying desire to get up off the couch and do something with it. With the responsibility of power comes the internal impetus to work it out in everyday life.

4. IT REQUIRES INTIMACY.

Intimacy is the most risky component of life. It means getting messy with someone. And intimacy with God is as messy and inconvenient as any human relationship we've ever had. But intimacy with God also results in a more beautiful reward than any relationship we've ever experienced.

5. IT MEANS OUR FOUNDATION IS GOD, NOT THE BIBLE.

Again, statements like this are sensitive for Evangelical conservatives and can come across as blasphemous. But here's the thing: Proper understanding of the Bible comes from an intimate relationship with God and the illumination of the Holy Spirit. The Bible can—to some degree—help us understand God. But as we all know, someone can be well-versed in the Bible yet miss God altogether. Viewing the Bible as prescription tempts us to experience it as a text, apart from relationship with God. But when we have an intimate and active relationship with the Holy Spirit, we have the ability to supernaturally understand what has been written.

6. WE LOSE CONTROL

All these things point to one underlying factor: When we expect the revelation of God in our lives, we lose control. We no longer have a God that we can contain within the box of our expectations and limitations. Rather, we understand that as He continues to reveal Himself and the nature of who we are in relationship with Him, life becomes wily and unpredictable. It means we are poised to receive and respond at every moment of everyday. It means we begin living lives of stories worth telling. We begin living lives beyond ourselves and the limitation of our own humanity. It means we begin seeing the kingdom come.

Of course this terrifies the leaders of our systems of control. If all this is true, power no longer resides only in the hands of a select few. Rather the work, move and communication of God are distributed throughout the Body of Christ—just as it was intended to be. As we are filled with the Holy Spirit and hear His voice, each of us who are filled with the Spirit step into a new level of effective life and thriving ministry.

But let's return to my friend, Carlos, whose life is committed to disturbing and disrupting the career Christians. He did this for a while, and, in his own words, people just thought he was a ass. He knew the solution wasn't to end his mission and put his voice to rest, but he also realized something was missing. That's when he added "for the sake of Christ" to the end of his mission statement.

His goal wasn't to disturb and disrupt simply to leave things a mess. Rather, he came to realize the power and beauty of loving like Jesus, during and after the process of stirring the pot.

The same must be true for us if we're going to recognize the revelations of God in our life. As we step into a more intimate relationship with God, such that we hear His voice and respond, we must do so in a way that loves people and reflects the hope of God for the universe. We mustn't perpetuate the Evangelical posture of destruction. No, we must proactively live to make the world look like heaven.

LIVING A BIBLICAL LIFE

For many of us, living a biblical life means learning what the saints of old said and doing what they told us to do. But living a biblical life is not only doing what the Bible says. It's living how those in the Bible lived. Let's go back to the story at the beginning of this chapter—the story of the Muslim man who saw Jesus. How would you and I respond to the lives and stories of the people in the Bible had we been introduced to them without the dogmas and additions of those between the last page of Revelation and today? If we had an encounter with Jesus through the pages of the Bible, and then a divine filling of the Holy Spirit, I suspect we would go into our neighborhoods with an expectation of living in that power. It's only through an attempt to theologically justify times of silence that we have begun to construct a different reality, apart from the reality we see lived out in their lives.

Which seems more Biblical: The Muslim cleric who wakes from a dream in which a man, calling himself Jesus, invites the cleric into a relationship; or a classroom full of Western Christians debating the merits of predestination and freewill? It's not to say there's no room for such a conversation. But if we've reduced our faith to the latter, we're missing the boat. That's why I think we've seen a burgeoning of "ministry schools" over the last decade. Christians are hungry, not only for a classroom experience, but to be activated in their spiritual gifts to live a life of power in the world.

Several summers ago, I was doing some work for an international para-church ministry. One of the speakers got up on stage and asked, "If we put our lives in the pages of the book of Acts, and people read it, what would they think?" Most likely, they'd be confused. Where's the power in this person's life? Where's the supernatural activity, the infilling, leadership, and manifestation of the Holy Spirit? People would be reading Acts. They'd read of the miracles of Peter and Paul. They'd read of the story of Pentecost. They'd hear of supernatural power. Then they'd get to a group of people who woke up every day, drove to work, went to the grocery store, woke up the next day, did it all again and once a week all got together to listen to one person talk about a bygone era of power and radical life change.

God is not dead. We've just put him in a box of silence. It's time to once again live a Biblical life. It's time to unbox an infinite God and listen to what's He's saying.

QUESTIONS AND CONVERSATIONS :

- Has God ever spoken something to you? How? What did you do with it?

- Do you think there are attributes of God that we have yet to discover? Do you think God wants us to know some of those things about who He is?

- Are there things that make you feel uneasy when it comes to the concept of divine revelation? What are those things? What do you think you should do with them?

DO SOMETHING :

Consistently spend time in a quiet place in the coming days with the intention of hearing God say something specific. Maybe it's something about God. Maybe it's something about you or your life. Maybe it's something about someone else. This process might take some time. Be willing to carve out time to hear God.

SPIRITUAL INNOVATION // CHAPTER EIGHT
EMBRACE INNOVATION

SPIRITUAL INNOVATION

My friend, Lander, likes to go to the woods. I'm somebody who thrives around people but Lander thrives by going away to the woods and walking around by himself. We live in the middle of a city, so I'm not even sure what woods he goes to, but when he goes to the woods, he seems to come back with something good. So, I'm okay with him driving away to nature every now and again.

One day, he came back with this.

Israel had been enslaved by the Egyptians. Moses was in the desert. God met him there and told him to go deliver the people. Eventually, after fear and insecurity and empowerment and miracles, signs and wonders, Moses and the people got on their way. It was an extravagant sight: a pillar of fire led them by night and a pillar of smoke by day. At times, when the Egyptian army would get too close to the Israelites (because they regretted letting them go and wanted to re-enslave them), the pillar of God's manifested presence, God's glory, would get behind the people and keep them safe from the Egyptians.

Then, the Israelites came to a sea and didn't know what to do. "Help us!" Moses cried out. "Alright. Get over there to the water, lift up your arms, and the sea will part," God said to Moses. Sure enough, it worked, and Israel escaped from the hands of the Egyptians. They were on their way to the Promised Land.

As the result of some poor decisions, they wandered around for 40 years. Eventually, they came to the Promised Land, but they were separated from it by the Jordan River. "God, we have a problem," Joshua—now the leader of the Israelites—said to God. "Remember the thing with Moses?" God asked. "We're going to do that again. It's time to part those waters." The waters were parted and once again, the people of Israel walked on the land between the parted waters.

Later, the prophet Elijah comes along. He is mentoring a guy named Elisha. They're walking and they encounter the Jordan River, just like Joshua before them. Both of them are well acquainted with the stories of the patriarchs, so they think, "When the people of God come to water, they part it." Putting a new twist on an old trick, Elijah takes off his cloak and strikes the water with it. Boom! The waters part. Elijah and Elisha get to the other side of the river, the waters close up, and the two of them walk on. Suddenly, a chariot of fire appears and takes Elijah up to heaven. In the process, that cloak falls from the sky back to earth. Elisha picks it up, walks back to the Jordan River, says, "Where now is the Lord, the God of Elijah?" and strikes the river. The waters part and Elisha walks back across on dry land.

Through Moses, God set a standard. Through Joshua he confirmed it. Elijah adopted it. Elisha mimicked it.

Several thousand years later, Jesus comes. He has just done the work of feeding the 5,000 and tells his disciples, "You guys get going. I'll catch up." Jesus dismisses the people and then goes up on a mountain to pray and spend time with the Father. The disciples had gone out on a boat. Wind was stirring up the waves and they were crashing against the boat. As dawn approached, Jesus wanted to get to the disciples. And although history had set the precedent of "when God's people need to get somewhere and water is in the way, they part it," Jesus doesn't part it. He walks on it.

Had Jesus parted the water, the disciples would have surely been amazed. But because Jesus came to them walking on the water, they were scared. Jesus was setting a new standard, and because it was new, the disciples were afraid of it.

We're all scared of things we don't understand. But what would happen if we began to live our lives expecting things outside of the ordinary from a God who exceeds our understanding, who is bigger than we can comprehend? What if we learned to innovate our spirituality, to keep up with a God who is infinitely creative?

INNOVATION ALL AROUND

A few years ago, I started taking improv classes at a theater here in Orlando. I had watched it so many times. I had always found it interesting. And honestly, when done well, I found it to be some of the best, most witty comedy I'd ever seen. So I gathered six friends I thought would enjoy it and we signed up for a class. Later, I took some intensive workshops. Most of the other students in the class were seasoned improvisors. It was intimidating and the teacher of the class expected quite a bit from us. He had us, two at a time, get up on stage and do scenes. Most of my time in those workshops consisted of me faking it—at least to the point of not letting the other actors in the room know I had actually never done this before. But after that workshop and subsequent hour-after-hour of scene work, things changed.

Later, I was in another weekend workshop intensive, and I had this moment of epiphany. We took turns on stage—half the class at a time. I was sitting and watching the other half of the class doing a scene and one of the actors said, "And that's why you'll never be president" to one of the other characters. After the scene was over, I asked the teacher, a long time professional improvisor—"If you were to say that line, would you completely conceptualize it in your mind and then speak it, or would you begin to speak it and see what flows out after it?"

He responded immediately. "Early on, as an improvisor, I would access my intellect. I am pretty smart. I'm well read. I can think of some good stuff. But that's limited. There's an end to that, and if that's what I count on, inevitably my improvisation will become stale. After about a year of conceptualizing everything I said, I got to the point where I would open my mouth—as the character—and just let whatever flowed out, flow out."

The more practice we have with something, the greater ability we have to operate and innovate within it.

So many Christians are in the constant process of accessing what they know. We've learned a lot about our faith and so we rely on that information, from the past, to inform our current decisions. That's why "Christian Education" has become such a sacred cow. The more we know, we believe, the better Christians we become. The best Christian is the one who has the most information crammed into his or her brain.

But even from a completely natural standpoint, Google has ushered us into an age where knowledge is no longer power. As we read in Chapter 6, the poorest people in America have immediate access to more information through cellular devices than Ronald Reagan had access to in 1981 as President of the United States. Information is ubiquitous and therefore the acquisition of it for the purpose of retention and power is largely ineffective. Today, even in the natural mind, we've realized power is not in knowing information. Power is in the ability to process existing information, apply it to our current reality, and predict what is next. We live, largely, in a prophetic culture.

We see it quite clearly in the realm of technology. Growing up, my family's first computer was an Apple IIe. It had a monochrome monitor and a tan body. The only color on the computer was the rainbow apple on the front of the machine. Of course, our family–like most Americans—abandoned the Apple brand in the 90s, but I accidentally stumbled back into the Apple domain in the early 2000s. I placed a bid on an Apple 667 mHz laptop on eBay, and actually won it. I stupidly went to the bank, got a cashiers check for nearly $2000, and mailed it to a stranger in another state. Luckily, internet tech scams were not yet in full swing, so a week or so later, I received

SPIRITUAL INNOVATION

a box in the mail with a computer running the first version of Mac OSX.

Initially, it didn't make much difference to me. "Whatever. It's a computer. I use it to do stuff." But (and here comes the most cliché statement I could make in a book like this) Apple captured my heart. Eventually, I was reading live blogs of Apple Keynote events. I wanted to know what was coming. What was next?! And—no joke—while watching Steve Jobs give a keynote presentation some time in the late 2000s, I found myself drawn to tears. It wasn't the result of marketing manipulation. I was genuinely inspired. Steve Jobs wasn't passionate about building a company or making a buck. In that keynote, I could see Steve Jobs was passionate about the user's experience. He had dedicated his life to asking, "How can we do this better than anyone else in the world?" And he did.

It all made sense a few years later when Andy Crouch published his article "Steve Jobs: The Secular Prophet" in the Wall Street Journal. In it, Andy observes, "Politically, militarily, economically, the decade was defined by disappointment after disappointment—but technologically, it was defined by a series of elegantly produced events in which Steve Jobs, commanding more attention and publicity each time, strode on stage with a miracle in his pocket." He notes Jobs was a man who would make a promise, and that promise would be fulfilled, on time, just as it was predicted.

While Christians are stuck in a cycle of reproduction and—at best—mimicry of some bygone era, the world is well at work innovating. Once we overcome our fear of the new, the unknown, we're able to build.

EARLY INNOVATORS

Peter was a shifty disciple. He denied Christ when things got rough.

EMBRACE INNOVATION

He didn't always have the right answers. Perhaps that's why he was such an innovator. He was a guy who wasn't afraid to make mistakes, and through him God did some heavy innovation. He was the guy who said, "Hey Jesus, if that's really you walking on the water, tell me to come to you." And because he was willing to take the risk, he was part of Spiritual Innovation—the movement from parting the waters to walking on them. In the parting of the water, we are taught we have dominion over the water. Peter had the ability to either replicate the event or build from the principle. He chose to build from the principal and it brought him closer to Jesus. We see this throughout the rest of the New Testament.

The disciples saw Jesus heal. Eventually, he sent them out to do some healing of their own. Some of it was successful. Some of it not. And through those less successful moments, Jesus taught the disciples how to operate in the principle of healing. As Jesus was preparing for his departure, he said, "You'll do the things you've seen me do. But not only that, you'll do things greater than these." In this, Jesus was saying, "Don't only replicate what you've seen me do. Take the principles and use them as the foundation for greater revelation of the kingdom. This is only the beginning, boys."

So Peter and the rest of the disciples, after receiving the Holy Spirit, begin the work of reconciliation. Because of the miraculous work of the Spirit through them, there is a massive influx of new believers in Jesus. They heal by prayer and laying on of hands, but then other things start happening. Early on in the book of Acts, it says, "people brought the sick into the streets and laid them on beds and mats so that at least Peter's shadow might fall on some of them as he passed by." The precedent was that people are healed by laying on of hands and prayer. But suddenly, Peter's shadow is passing over people and they are being healed. It was a new standard.

And the innovation continues throughout Acts. While on his way to round up Christians to be persecuted, Paul has a transforming encounter with God. Immediately after, he begins operating in the miraculous. Inevitably, he had heard the rumors of the healings performed by Jesus, but they weren't a limitation to him. They were a standard to be exceeded. And exceed them, he did. Acts 19 records, "God did extraordinary miracles through Paul, so that even handkerchiefs and aprons that had touched him were taken to the sick, and their illnesses were cured and the evil spirits left them."

While on a retreat, I stayed up late one night with a friend. He believes in the power of the Holy Spirit and that God is alive and active in our lives. The conversation turned to discussing some of the ways people are seeing the manifestation of the Holy Spirit in modern times.

"Some of these things that are happening today—I don't see them happening in the Bible and I'm skeptical of their veracity," he eventually said.

"Can you imagine if the disciples would have operated that way?" I asked incredulously. "If they would have said, 'We don't see it in the scriptures' or even 'Jesus didn't do that, so it must not be from God.' They would have missed out on miracle after miracle, opportunity after opportunity!"

And how true that is. The accounts of the lives of the patriarchs and prophets and apostles and saints in the Bible represent one surprising new reality after another, and yet for some reason, we've settled for far less. Not only have we settled for it, we've created new theologies to reinforce it. But God is calling the Church back into a new era of accelerated Spiritual Innovation. God wants to make up for the years the enemy has stolen and propel us into a greater deluge of revelation and "Thy kingdom come" than the world has ever seen before.

DISCERNING COMMUNALLY

Those of us in American Evangelical culture often view moments of conversion as more of an end than a beginning. We work hard to "lead someone to Christ" and once achieved, we take the position of, "Great, that's done." Of course we know the value of life-long growth and discipleship. Certainly there is often a desire for that. But even our models of discipleship are often built around the end of something—the fleshly man- more than they're built around cultivating the spiritual man.

Because of this, we don't have a framework for—or even more difficult, we have an opposition toward—the concept of Spiritual Innovation. We don't anticipate God will continue to speak to us and through us as we grow and mature in Him, so we don't have a framework for discerning the spirits together.

As I've talked with friends, scholars, and spiritual advisors about some of the things in this chapter, I have heard several times, "well, I'm scared that…" and you can fill in the blanks with any number of concerns that follow. Let me say this: I understand the fear. But I am also confident fear is not a reason to avoid something. Fear is not from the Lord and that fear is certainly not a reason to not move forward or take a risk. The ultimate result of fear is immobilization, that's why I think scripture makes it clear: "God gave us a spirit not of fear but of power and love and self-control." (2 Timothy 1:7 ESV)

"Well, caution then," they say. "Caution because of things like Mormonism, belief systems in which people are adding on…"

"Ah! Yes!" I remind them, "That's why discerning communally is important!"

In our current context, we don't have a framework by which people hear from God and, subsequently, engage in a process with their community. This process of communal discernment is the process by which we have today's New Testament. The Council of Trent canonized the scriptures for Catholicism in 1546, and the foundation for the canonization of the Protestant scriptures was laid as part of the Westminster Confession of Faith in 1647.

But our unwillingness to have conversations about the issue altogether has led us to a different place. Today, we have no process of mutual submission. Therefore, there are three common scenarios.

1. Instances like that of Joseph Smith, in which an individual has some sort of encounter and presents it to others for individual, personal acceptance or rejection. "I have this word. You can believe it, and come be part of what I'm starting, or reject it and not be part of this." Therefore, there's no room for conversation or correction. Simply an attitude of "I heard something and I'm outta here."

2. The Pope. In this case, there is predetermined, broad acceptance that the declarations of a single individual immediately, and without question, hold a position of spiritual authority superior to others and accepted as the words of God. There is no room for question or conversation because the people have already surrendered their willingness and responsibility to test together.

3. "Thus saith the Lord" is a popular phrase in some protestant circles who still hold to the possibility that God is speaking and revealing. In this scenario, it's usually acceptable for any "spirit-filled" individual to exercise the priesthood of the believer. There's an openness and belief that the Holy Spirit can empower any believer to be a steward of the revelation of God. But, there's usually little room for challenge. The attitude is often, "God said it. I've told you. Receive it."

All three of these scenarios have something in common: they don't recognize the value of the collective church discerning together.

In 1 Corinthians 14:29-30, on the heels of Paul's mention of apocalypses as a means by which the Church is strengthened, he says, "Let two or three prophets speak, and let the others weigh what is said. If a revelation is made to another sitting there, let the first be silent." It was Paul's expectation that communal discernment of revelation would be a regular part of orderly worship.

He reaffirms this in 1 Thessalonians 5:20-21. "Do not despise prophecies, but test everything; hold fast what is good." Not only does he reaffirm the process of testing, he acknowledges that we won't hit the mark 100% of the time.

Another unifying factor of the three scenarios above is an expectation of "rightness." This is the underlying belief that "we shouldn't test what has been said, because the person saying it is already correct." In order for us to practice apocalypses in a healthy way, one of the present factors must be humility. Not only should the collective Body recognize their role in discernment together, those who speak must do so with humility and a willingness to mutually submit to one another.

This culture of mutual submission and humility not only leads us toward more clearly discerning the voice of God. It also creates an environment of grace—an environment in which each of us has the opportunity to say, "I sense God saying this." Then, we engage in love together to use godly wisdom to test. We become excited to experiment. We don't respond harshly out of a spirit of fear. Rather, we search the depths of God together in love. We are expectant that together, we will encounter new aspects of His character and deeper levels of His wisdom. As we take on this expectation, we begin to truly discover an infinite God.

SPIRITUAL INNOVATION

QUESTIONS AND CONVERSATIONS :

- Is most of your faith stuck mimicking things you've seen exemplified elsewhere? Are you open to seeing God do something unique in and through you? Have you ever experienced that before? What was it like?

- Are there risks you don't take in your life-specifically in your spiritual life-out of fear? What are those fears? How can you move beyond them?

- What might a culture of discerning communally look like? How can we operate with wisdom and humility as we move alongside people of faith around us?

DO SOMETHING :

Spiritual Innovation begins with the foundation of understanding what has existed in the past. We cannot innovate without first knowing what we're building upon. Take some time to look at the miracles of Jesus in the New Testament as well as the works of the early Church in the book of Acts. This week, take a risk. Find an opportunity to practice one of those miracles. When you see the opportunity, step into the moment with faith and remember the miracles of the past that serve as a foundation for moving forward.

Here's the thing. There's no guarantee that you'll experience the miracle. But, it's establishing this habit that moves us into a life of innovation. The more we try, the more success we see. Let this "do something" be the beginning of a new habit in your life.

SPIRITUAL INNOVATION // CHAPTER NINE
DISCOVER THE INFINITE GOD

SPIRITUAL INNOVATION

Donia and I have had a long standing relationship. She's a hip girl. I enjoy our regular rendezvous. We met one another in the early part of the 2000s. I was looking for a place to get my hair cut and someone told me about this place in a pretty great part of town called Ivanhoe Village. So, I walked in and asked, "I need a hair cut. Is anyone available?"

"Sure. Hold on. I think Donia is available."

My entire life my parents had taken me to a tiny barber shop—four barber's chairs tightly packed into one room. Opposite the barber's chairs was a row of mismatched seats where people waited for the next available barber. The primary hair-cutting tool was a pair of electric clippers used to cut through one man's (or boy's) hair after another. At best, it was an efficient assembly line set up to accomplish a purely utilitarian process that seemed to be nothing more than a nuisance—even to those barbers, who made their living $7 at a time.

Eventually, I moved on to a series of strip mall joints. This time, labeled "salon," but it seemed these big-box hair stores were pretty much like the barber shop, only with gel.

So, I was in my early twenties and ready for something else. That's when I met Donia. I didn't know what to think but she had magical hands. She didn't just wash hair. She massaged like a champ. So, together, we embarked on what has become a decade-long hair odyssey involving various shapes, lengths and states of asymmetry. Donia is an adventurer and amazing at what she does. So, I was willing to become her co-creator, my head the canvas.

But Donia isn't just an adventurer in her job or art form. What I have learned about Donia is that she has a spirit of discovery oozing throughout all her life. We've had some interesting conversations about God in our times together. During one of those recent conversations, I realized something. Her spirit of discovery, when it comes to God, is beautiful. She and I might not always land on the same page, and we've certainly had very different experiences, but something that unifies us is the fact that we're both always looking.

It seems so contrary to how I was raised to posture myself in this way when it comes to God. The way I was raised was to say: "This is what's right. This is the totality of it. Don't let anyone tell you differently. Set up a fort of ideology and defend it with your life." In order to maintain this kind of control over my theology, I had to put aside my childhood mystic. I had to become what I referred to as a realist (but what was probably a cynic). All the while, there were glimpses of my true nature.

In my sixth grade English class, we read "A Wrinkle In Time." I loved it. So, when I discovered the author, Madeleine L'Engle, had written a book on art, I drove to the book store and picked up "Walking On Water: Reflections on Faith and Art." In it, Madeleine (I use her first name because that's what it seems she'd want. She doesn't seem like a last name kind of lady) writes this:

"There is nothing so secular that it cannot be sacred, and that is one of the deepest messages of the Incarnation."

It was this simple phrase that completely changed the way I posture myself toward everything. I just couldn't be a cynic anymore after reading this. It seemed too contrary to my true nature.

Some Christians love to define themselves as "broken" or "dirty," over and over again. But in this simple statement, Madeleine reminded me, as she reminds us all, that there is nothing beyond the scope of redemption, thanks to Christ. God, who is perfect, came and dwelt in an earthen vessel made of human flesh, and in so doing, revealed to all creation the truth that is so difficult for us to grasp: there is nothing not redeemable.

SPIRITUAL INNOVATION

While humanity has neglected the divine image within, God has not forgotten it.

GOD IS EVERYWHERE

One afternoon, I was sitting with my friend, Chris, eating lunch. He was a new friend and I was already seeing things he believed about himself that were keeping him from stepping into the fullness of who He was in Christ. Around the same time, God was revealing some things to me about my prophetic gift. In the past, I had noticed things in people and, without consideration, called them out. But God had been teaching me that simply because something was true didn't mean it was supposed to be said. In fact, discovering truth is often the beginning of something, not the end.

So, I began asking God, "You've given me the ability to see things as they could be. Give me the means to help them get there." And He responded with this: "Don't tell people and things how they DON'T look like me. Tell them how they DO look like me."

Woah!

It was God saying, "There is nothing so secular that it cannot be sacred, and that is one of the deepest messages of the Incarnation" and then taking it one step further. "Everyone around you already has a bit of me in them. I'm already working in them. I'm already present with them. You're just invited along for the journey. Find me in them and encourage it. By so doing, you'll nurture them to a place of wanting to embody and reflect more of me."

So, in that moment, sitting across from Chris, I asked, "Lord, how does Chris embody you? How are you already working in him? And how can I speak those things out?" I listened. I looked. Then, I called out the traces of God I saw in Chris. He was able to receive and be encouraged by those things rather than, once again, having someone tell him what they perceived to be wrong with him. Chris left our conversation affirmed in the glimpses of the image of God inside him.

Chris is a believer and we might expect to see the image of God in those following Christ. But, in Athens, Paul found God in unexpected places. In Acts 17, Paul, while preaching to the Jews and believing Greeks, was overheard by some philosophers. They were intrigued by what he was saying and invited him to speak in the Areopagus—a place where new ideas were listened to and discussed by the Athenians. When he got there, Paul could have railed against the altars and idols throughout the city. He could have talked about the practices he found immoral. But, instead, he found the presence of God in their culture and practices and drew it out as the foundation of his verbal treatise.

People of Athens! I see that in every way you are very religious. For as I walked around and looked carefully at your objects of worship, I even found an altar with this inscription: to an unknown god. So you are ignorant of the very thing you worship—and this is what I am going to proclaim to you.

"Here's God in your midst. You're worshipping him, but there's so much more of this Unknown God to know!" Paul says. And he goes on to quote two of their very own philosophers.

'For in him we live and move and have our being.' As some of your own poets have said, 'We are his offspring.'

Paul's ability to see the nature and character of God revealed in and through these people was limited only to his willingness and posture.

We miss the boat if we reduce what's happening here to the cliché conversation of cultural relevance. I am not advocating for the inclusion of movie clips in our worship (nor am I opposed to it) or for manipulating the latest television reality series logo into a Christian slogan or church message series (although I would oppose that). What I'm saying is that inherent in the icons and rituals of our culture are glimpses of the divine nature in us.

I'm suggesting the posture of the Christian should not be *against* culture with the idea that we are sent to "redeem" it. Rather, the assumption should be God is already at work around us—we have simply been given eyes to see that movement. In fact, we have not only been given eyes to see it, but to bring it to light, join it, and cultivate it.

What would it look like for you to discover where God is present and at work in and through those around you—and how can you join the movement?

MONOPOLY BREAKERS

Christians have taken the view—at least in my limited experience—that we have a monopoly on God's presence. We've been taught God only shows up in things branded "Christian."

All the time, people were telling Jesus what they thought he should do and where they thought he should go. In Mark 3, he had begun his public ministry and was going from town to town, healing and teaching. He had appointed his disciples and ends up at a house with them. The house is surrounded by people who want to see and hear Jesus. At first, his ministry wasn't that big of a deal for those around him because it wasn't so public. But now, this was getting uncomfortable for his family.

Then Jesus entered a house, and again a crowd gathered, so that he and his disciples were not even able to eat. When his family heard about this, they went to take charge of him, for they said, "He is out of his mind."

Jesus's family didn't know what to do with his ministry once it grew beyond something they could understand; and I don't think we are much different.

We serve an infinite God, but infinity scares us. The things we cannot quantify and contain are out of our control, and—as we've discussed at length—the chief end of the flesh is control. So, we create systems to contain and define the uncontainable and indefinable. Any words we use to describe God are, in the end, a reduction of the totality of who He is. That doesn't mean there are not components of God He desires for humanity to know. In fact, I'd suggest God is continuously revealing more of Himself, in increasing amounts, in surprising places.

The point is God can't be perfectly defined. He can't be put in a box; and for all our efforts to get Him there, we're making Him in our own image.

Regardless of what kind of boxes we want to put around God, God goes where he wants and he does what he wants. We only have two options. 1. Ignore it. or 2. Participate in it.

Mondays are my sabbath rest. Coming off a weekend of teaching or leading worship at our church gatherings and being surrounded by lots of people, it's good to spend some time in quiet. Most Mondays, for the last several years, I've taken an hour to listen to the previous weekend's episode of *This American Life*. Each week on *This American Life*, host Ira Glass and other contributors choose a theme and bring a variety of 10-25 minute stories on that theme. There have been some Mondays when I have asked myself, "Should I listen to a sermon from Pastor X instead of listening to *This American Life*? I mean, wouldn't that be the spiritual thing to do on my day off?" It's a clear example of spiritual monopoly-ism. It's the belief that I will more likely find God in an overt spiritual experience like a sermon, than in the stories of *This American Life*—a show hosted by a self-proclaimed atheist. And yet inevitably, when I put my headphones in and embark on a walk through the neighborhood, God surprises me by showing up in the stories of *This American Life*.

God is all over the place and, if we are willing to open our eyes to that reality, we gain the ability to see him everywhere. I was sitting at lunch with a guy recently. He too labels himself an atheist (along with Ira Glass). He broke open a fortune cookie, read the fortune, and showed it to me. "Happiness is everywhere, but not everyone sees it." Later, we got to talking about spiritual things. "You know that fortune you showed me," I asked. "That's how I feel about God. I look everywhere, and there He is."

When we recognize the ability to see God all over, we begin recognizing him in places others find void of Him.

A couple years ago, a particular movie was popular in my circle of friends who were questioning who God is and the validity of Jesus. They were posting it online, so I watched it. The "documentary" attempts to discredit Christianity by drawing parallels between the account of Jesus—his life, virgin birth, death and resurrection—to other religions and stories from around the world. It talks about how the origins of world religions come from a value and love for the sun, stars and planets. The film attempts to use the ubiquity of good versus evil, resurrection and events in other religions which parallel the birth and life of Jesus as evidence against the deity of Christ.

In our current construct and posture, in which Christianity is the only vehicle through which God may reveal truth, the prevalence of these spiritual concepts do, indeed, seem to be at odds with the Christian monopoly. But what happens when we shift our posture just slightly?

At the time of Jesus' birth, we know magi came from the east. These non-Jewish men sought a king they knew would be revealed by a celestial event. Is it possible that, through the stories of eastern mythologies, these men were made aware of the coming king? Additionally, is it possible the Egyptian stories of a sun god, conceived of a virgin, who died and was resurrected (although the exact details of the resurrection story of Horace are in dispute), are not actually in conflict with the message of Jesus but a divine message provided as a prophetic foretelling of the coming Christ?

Christians raised with a monopolistic perspective find these realities disheartening and even threatening to the core of their belief, which requires an expectation of a single means by which God reveals truth. But if we take a view similar to Paul's, we see these stories and belief systems as prophetic introductions to the fulfillment of them in Christ.

In John 6, Jesus says, "No one can come to me unless the Father who sent me draws them." In other words, there must be a divine encounter prior to an individual becoming a "Christian." Additionally, if God has revealed Himself through nature as we see Paul state in Romans 1, then certainly there is a possibility for revelation of the nature and character of God *outside* the realm of Christian doctrine. In fact, if every good and perfect gift comes from God, then we have glimpsed the goodness of God in the gifts and experiences of our lives, right? Don't we even see God's character in the birth of a child or the celebration of marriage?

Let me make an important distinction here. This is not a pluralist viewpoint. My friend Ryan had great insight as we talked about this idea. He said, "It's not bowing down to another throne. It's being willing to open our eyes to the presence of God throughout the earth." If Paul was able to find Jehovah in the polytheistic religion of the Athenians, shouldn't we be able to find him in our lives and communities as well?

SPIRITUAL INNOVATION

And this doesn't negate the proclamation of the good news of Jesus. It just shifts how we approach people. We don't assume people haven't experienced God. Rather, we discover how they *have* and allow that to point to Jesus.

EXPECT TO SEE

In 2009, I attended a "God Debate" in Orlando. Thousands of Christians and Atheists packed the UCF Arena ready to hear the discourse between Dinesh D'Souza and Christopher Hitchens. It was a polite environment. No yelling. No uproarious booing. Each of the two men would make a statement, usually followed by polite clapping by one demographic and respectful silence by the other. I didn't take a poll, but it seemed those who came in believing in God, left believing in God. And those who came in not believing in God, left not believing in God. I'm not railing against the conversation. There was value in it happening and in my being there. I only set up this scene to ask a question: Why was it a debate? Why was the entire conversation framed in the context of one person being correct and the other being incorrect?

When any ideology positions itself in opposition to another, it misses a huge opportunity to say the words, "You're right, and..." These might be some of the most important words Christians can speak. They take us from a position of "I'm right, and when you agree with me, I'll accept you" to "I'll meet you where you are and invest in taking a journey with you". It postures us to look for God and bring to light His presence and power already at work in the world.

Do you remember the story I told in chapter 7—about my friends Sam and Kristen hosting the night of prayer and encouragement, where several people spoke the same words of encouragement over me in the same evening? That night started with Sam asking each person in the room to talk about some of the ways they hear God.

Some people talked about seeing visions or having dreams. Others talked about having a sense or leading. As we went around the circle, I was pondering the question. It was my turn.

"I see and hear God in unexpected places. He shows me things about Himself and His heart and me and us through things people often relegate to the category of 'unspiritual.' I'm thankful for that. I'm thankful I can sit in the bar at the Grand Bohemian Hotel in downtown Orlando, writing this book, and at any moment, I can look up and see Him. I see Him in the laughs of the people having conversation. I see Him in the smile of the bartender. I see Him in the generosity of a friend buying another friend a drink. And I feel Him in me—in the compassion I have for the person sitting alone.

I think that's why Madeleine L'Engle's quote means so much to me. It has opened my spiritual and physical eyes to seeing Him in everything, in every situation. When I'm willing, when I want to, He's right there, ready to be seen.

UNBOX THE INFINITE

One evening, I was sitting in the front living room of my house with my friend, Ethan. It was unusually quiet. My five roommates were all out of the house and the weather had yet to heat up enough to necessitate the incessant hum of the window AC unit. The orange glow of the incandescent porch lights shined through the front widow and dimly lit the room.

"I had this dream once," Ethan said. I nodded. "It starts out kinda weird. I was walking through a mall with a group of friends and there was a war going on outside. I think I had played *Call of Duty* just before bed. Anyway, a hand grenade came through the window of one of the stores and landed near my group of friends. I jumped on the bomb, and it exploded, killing me. Then, I went to heaven. It was so strange. I didn't even know I was there at first. It was like I was at a club of some sort—like sitting with a bunch of people at a bar. Then suddenly, an alarm went off. Everyone started walking out of the bar across these bridges that emanated in every direction, so I followed them. We all filed into completely white classrooms and I started asking everyone what we were doing there. No one would really answer me. Then, this instructor came in. He looked at me, with a look of perplexity and anger, and he asked me, "Why do you think you'd stop learning just because you got to heaven?"

Ah! Yes! What an awesome question.

"How could there ever be an end to discovering an infinite God?!" I asked, rhetorically.

Of course, there are lots of questions related to the unknown nature of heaven, time and eternity that throw a wrench in the literality of Ethan's dream and, subsequently, my question. For instance, "learning" implies chronological time. And, if time doesn't exist in heaven, what would the nature of "learning" or "discovery" be? How could I learn something I didn't know previously if there is no "before" or "after" at all?

But, if God is infinite, then there is no end to our discovery of Him. Since our current human state prevents us from grasping the complexities of eternity, let's ask the same question in light of today, here on earth.

"How could there ever be an end to discovering an infinite God?!"

I've talked quite a bit about Christian movements of the present and the past—mostly in the context of the Reformation and American Evangelicalism. It's easy to look back on these movements and see what's broken about them. But, for our purposes and in the context of the message of this book, it is also important to recognize their contributions. Because both the Reformation and American Evangelicalism can be examples of Spiritual Innovation. They have both served beneficial purposes in helping us come to a different understanding of God and our relationship to Him.

The Reformation, for instance, was instrumental in pointing out and championing the priesthood of the believer. In large part, the Catholic church at the time had created dogmas determining who could communicate with God, as well as when and where that communication could happen. But the Reformation brought about a revelation and accentuation of the role of the individual in cultivating a personal intimacy with God—direct access to Him.

For those who were alive during that time period—Martin Luther and so many others— that was Spiritual Innovation.

American Evangelicalism, too, has contributed some great things throughout its history: an increase in cultural engagement, thousands of people introduced to the message of Christ and an emphasis on global missions. Although it's easy to see the brokenness in these or even to dismiss them completely, these momentary expressions of Christianity have served an important role. For those who conceptualized and created these movements, that was Spiritual Innovation.

The problem comes when there is a tendency of these movements to see themselves as the last necessary and most pure iteration of whatever they represent—in this case, Christianity. There is a human tendency to become so indoctrinated by our own dogmas, we convince ourselves they stand alone as ultimate truth. There's a difference between the eternal, saving power of Jesus and the things we select (or are led into) as points of focus from one generation, season, movement, or moment of innovation to the next. Growth necessitates change in focus.

SPIRITUAL INNOVATION

I once was an Evangelical but am no longer. I don't hate Evangelicals. I don't think they're wrong or stupid. And I don't run away from those who are Evangelical to start my "own thing" in a spirit of rebellion.

And yet I make the statement above for two reasons:

First, it is so I can now ask: "how did you feel when you read that?" Maybe you felt excited because it's something you've wanted to say for a long time and have just been waiting for someone else to say it first. Maybe you felt sad because you're thinking, "oh, the poor boy has strayed away." It's that second response that worries me because it embodies a tight-fisted posture that is damaging to any movement. I hope we, as Christians, can begin to move away from it.

The reality is, it's a movement toward God that has brought me to a new place, not a movement away from Him. If you are too attached to your cause or movement (Evangelicalism or something else) it would be hard for you to see, but that's partially my point. When we're trying to protect our movement, we're saddened when people step into something else, even when that something else is more of God.

The second reason I make the statement is to help shape the conversation in a healthy way. I work at a church and I love the church. I'm not abandoning Jesus, or Christianity, when I say I'm not an Evangelical anymore. I'm simply shedding light on the new places God is taking me. I think people on all sides of the conversation need to see this is possible: you don't have to abandon God to dissociate from a movement. Inevitably, with time and coming generations, more people will make the same statement—and it's important we each have the freedom to do so.

There are those who have cherished the politicized, conservative, American Evangelical movement to the point they see it as the most pure, fully-realized form of Christianity. And because of that, there is a spirit of protectionism, of idolatry. If this is you, I want to say: I love you. I care for you. I'm thankful for you. You've laid a foundation for those of us who come behind you. Now it's time to champion your children. It's time to tell them to expect more. It's time to free them into the abundance of an infinite God and a thriving life in Christ. It's time to see an increased movement of the power of the Holy Spirit and the coming of the kingdom.

Together, we can look forward and believe for a unified, powerful Church built on the foundation of Christ. Together, we can step into more of Him. But "together" is a choice we all have to make, and protectionism is an enemy of "together."

It's easy to maintain by protecting, but God's not interested in maintenance. God is passionate about growth - the growth of His Church and the increase of His glory.

How is God going to grow his church? The same way he always has: through the revelation of His character to and through each individual. What would it look like for you to be on the lookout for such revelation, to adopt a spirit of discovery?

THE SPIRIT OF DISCOVERY

As we learn to see God, it's time we learn an important lesson from science: the spirit of discovery.

In the 5th century BC there were—in Greek culture—those who considered themselves atomists. They believed all matter—everything that existed—was made of atoms and voids. They didn't have microscopes to see what they believed. They only had their eyes, their observation of the world, and their subsequent philosophical understanding. For 2,400 years, this was the accepted belief—that atoms were the smallest building block of all matter. But between 1897 and

SPIRITUAL INNOVATION

1920, scientists discovered atoms were comprised of smaller particles: the electron, the neutron, and the proton. And while it took 2,400 years to discover these smaller particles, it only took scientists an additional 46 years to discover even smaller building blocks. In 1964, two scientists independently proposed the existence of the quark.

Scientists could have accepted the atom theory and ended their search. They could have stopped searching after the discovery of particles. Even today, scientists could say, "quarks are certainly the smallest building blocks of matter" and stop looking. But they don't. Scientists, committed to the spirit of discovery, continue to search for new realities. They don't stop asking "what's next." Instead they press on, always believing there's more.

The main thing the American Church can learn from science is the spirit of discovery. Don't stop searching. There's always more.

That's the spirit of revelation Paul prays for the Ephesians to encounter. That's the disclosure of truth concerning things before unknown. That's what Paul spoke of in his own life; and I would argue it's what Paul would want for us in our lives. That's what sparked the salvation and infilling of the Gentile believers. It's what allowed John to pen his revelation. And it's what Paul includes in his list of elements used to strengthen the body—The Church. God has offered us the opportunity to be recipients of His Revelation. Have you experienced that? Or are you simply mimicking the revelations of those around you? God is as alive today as He has ever been. He's simply waiting for us to move from merely believing and into a place of receiving His Revelation.

THE POWER OF MYSTERY

Somehow, Science and Christianity have gotten into a feud—a feud fueled by the obsession with the concrete. Christians say, "It must be God if you can't explain it." And scientists say, "If we can explain it, it must not be God." But just because something manifests itself in the physical doesn't mean it's not spiritual.

This tension between the known and unknown is what X-Files was about, one episode after the next, for nine seasons. Agent Mulder believed in the paranormal—the existence of ghosts, UFOs, monsters, and mutants; and the FBI sent Agent Scully to debunk Mulder's work on the X-Files. The two of them had similar experiences, walked away and filtered the information through their existing paradigms. Mulder's conclusion was: I can't explain them, so they must be supernatural. Scully's was: here's how I can explain it, so it must be confined to the realm of the natural.

In 2012, I heard an interview on NPR's *Fresh Air* between the host, Terry Gross and her guest, Susannah Cahalan. Cahalan had just released her book about an experience lasting several years, in which she "began to experience seizures, hallucinations, increasingly psychotic behavior and even catatonia." She was scared, as were her friends and family. At one point in the interview, Cahalan notes the similarities between her symptoms and the symptoms of cases of reported demon possession throughout history.

"When you think about the symptoms—in my case alone, this grandiosity, this violence. In a lot of children, you see hyper-sexuality. Even my grunts and these guttural sounds that came from me sounded superhuman to someone who might be inclined to think that way. ... When you see videos of people—in fact, when I see videos of myself—demonic possession is not far from your mind. It wasn't far from Stephen's mind when he first saw that seizure. And I've talked to many people who've had this disease, and one woman I spoke to actually asked for a priest because she said, 'The devil is inside of me. I need it out.' A little girl was grunting—they had a monitor in her room—and she was grunting so unnaturally that her parents looked at each other

and said, 'Is she, is she possessed?' They actually said that about a little girl. You can see throughout history why people would believe this." (11/14/2012 http://m.npr.org/news/Arts+%26+Life/165115921)

There's this unspoken sense throughout the interview of, "since we were able to diagnose the illness and treat it with medicine, it obviously wasn't spiritual in nature, and it's possible that we might be able to extrapolate my situation to cases reported to be demon possession in the past." Of course, I am NOT saying that Cahalan was possessed by a demon. But what I want to point out is the conventional thought that diagnosable and treatable illnesses cannot be tied to spiritual roots. Instead, there are often unseen factors—spiritual factors—that manifest themselves physically.

I loved Scooby Doo growing up. It hearkens back to the stories of the childhood mystic I talked about in the first chapter of this book. I loved the mysterious component. I loved the ghosts and monsters. But in writing this book, I realized this: Scooby Doo, while about the supernatural on the surface, actually teaches us from a young age that, if it can be explained, it must not be spiritual. At the end of every episode, they catch the monster, pull off his mask and reveal the true, human identity of the haunt. Next comes a detailed explanation of how each of the illusions were achieved through the use of projectors or mirrors or record players or electronic devices. But what Scooby Doo doesn't ask is: "What caused the human to want to steal or deceive in the first place?" Because while we can observe and explain all the external realities we want, we can't dismiss the spiritual component of the conversation. There's something going on beneath the surface.

What's interesting is that—in the Christianity/Science conversation—the debate is not about mystery and fact. The debate is about the rigid dogmas of modern Evangelicalism and modern science. But rigidity isn't helpful in either scenario. Both science and life in Christ require an expectation of more.

Both require an embracing of the unknown and a value for the invisible.

One thing I love about the scientific process is that it is rooted in creativity and mystery. There's a necessary element of curiosity in the heart of the scientist. Even if the end goal is empirical data, the starting point is the imagination—the hypothesis. Even if the hypothesis is rooted in prior knowledge and observation, there is still a willingness on the part of the researcher to embrace the unknown and dive in head first. There is an explorer's spirit, deep within the scientist, that has the potential to serve as inspiration in the spiritual realm. What if we each approached our spiritual lives the way a scientist faces an experiment—with an expectation for the discovery of more? What if we stepped out with hope?

While science seems to define itself by the absolute (simply building upon one observation after the other), scientists experience surprises quite frequently. The pacemaker, vulcanized rubber, plastic, dye, radioactivity, teflon, and the microwave oven were all discovered unexpectedly. Penicillin is, perhaps, one of the more famous stories of accidental discovery. In 1928, Alexander Fleming went on vacation without cleaning up his workstation. Upon returning, he noticed a fungus in some of his cultures. And yet, surprisingly, bacteria wasn't growing on the cultures. After some research, he discovered penicillin. Here is what he had to say about it:

"When I woke up just after dawn on September 28, 1928, I certainly didn't plan to revolutionize all medicine by discovering the world's first antibiotic, or bacteria killer. But I suppose that was exactly what I did." (Haven, Kendall F. (1994). Marvels of Science : 50 Fascinating 5-Minute Reads. Littleton, Colo: Libraries Unlimited. p. 182. ISBN 1-56308-159-8.)

Not only is surprise part of scientific discovery, so is creativity. HG Wells, Jules Verne, Arthur C. Clarke, Ray Bradbury—there's no doubt the fictional accounts of these science fiction writers have influenced scientists and scientific discovery. Verne, for instance, painted vivid pictures of travelers into the unknown—both into outer space and into the depths of the ocean—long before humanity was able to accomplish such feats. Both have now become a reality.

Today, scientists continue to investigate and move toward bringing science fiction into reality. In 2012, NASA announced work on faster-than-light-speed travel—the kind of travel that allowed the Star Trek crew to "boldly go where no man has gone before." This is the kind of travel that makes the dots of stars turn into long, white streaks. Additionally, NASA is working on a project that creates "a 'warp bubble' that moves space-time around the object, effectively re-positioning it" from Florida to California or from Earth to the outer stretches of the galaxy. Suspended animation, teleportation and Mars colonies are also science fiction ideas now in process.

(http://techland.time.com/2012/09/19/nasa-actually-working-on-faster-than-light-warp-drive/#ixzz2Q7aSBcgg)

As modern, western Christianity has attempted to respond to the rigidity of science, it has become rigid in itself. In an attempt to bring validation in the eyes of an increasingly scientific world, Christians have rejected the value of surprise and creativity, but both of these attributes remain an important and regular part of modern science. In the same way, they must be reclaimed as part of the Christian experience—as they have been from the beginning. Our spirituality, our revelation of God, can't be the same without them.

QUESTIONS AND CONVERSATIONS :

- Have you put limitations on how God may choose to reveal Himself? Why? What are those limitations?

- Have you ever encountered God in an unexpected place or thing? Where or what was it? How did you see God?

- Do you have a spirit of discovery about your faith? Do you expect to encounter God in new and unexpected ways? How do you (or how can you) practice that?

DO SOMETHING:

Find God in the unexpected. Listen to a song, read a story, look at a picture, go people watching, have a conversation with someone different than you. As you do one or more of these things, ask, "God, where are you in this?" Point it out to someone or share what you see with a friend.

SPIRITUAL INNOVATION // CHAPTER TEN
THE POWER OF LANGUAGE

If we're going to be spiritually innovative—to be curious and creative—we have to think about the language we use and don't use. Spiritual Innovation is tied to the spirit of discovery and expectation, and our vocabulary, the language we use, is integrally attached to our ability to think and dream. Even as we move from the realm of the metaphysical to the realm of the physical, the words we use matter. The tongue has the ability to shift and change an environment. What if there are concepts and realities God wants to reveal, but we don't even have language for them yet?

I went through a dystopian novel phase in the mid 2000s. I read Fahrenheit 451, Anthem, Brave New World and 1984 back to back. I was struck by George Orwell's thoughts on language in 1984. Later, in "'The Principles of Newspeak' An appendix to 1984," Orwell expresses the ability to limit thought and action by systematically designing and deconstructing language.

The purpose of Newspeak was not only to provide a medium of expression for the world-view and mental habits proper to the devotees of IngSoc, but to make all other modes of thought impossible. It was intended that when Newspeak had been adopted once and for all and Oldspeak forgotten, a heretical thought—that is, a thought diverging from the principles of IngSoc—should be literally unthinkable, at least so far as thought is dependent on words. Its vocabulary was so constructed as to give exact and often very subtle expression to every meaning that a Party member could properly wish to express, while excluding all other meaning and also the possibility of arriving at them by indirect methods. This was done partly by the invention of new words, but chiefly by eliminating undesirable words and stripping such words as remained of unorthodox meanings, and so far as possible of all secondary meaning whatever.

We live in a culture that limits conversation in the way we speak, the words we use, the concepts we're willing to discuss and the questions we're willing to ask. Even in this book, I've used words and asked questions that will, perhaps, make people uncomfortable.

This is not because they're inappropriate or vulgar but simply because, in asking a question, we can potentially unsteady a tightly held belief. We can open ourselves up to entirely new possibilities. Both realities can feel terrifying and out of our control.

But language, and our willingness to engage a new vocabulary, are essential in discovering new concepts and realities. They're essential to Spiritual Innovation.

LANGUAGE AND PERCEPTION

There's an amazing radio show from WNYC called RadioLab (I highly recommend the episodes "Emergence" and "Musical Language"). I listen to it on a regular basis and am always inspired. They get credit for this next story. They did the hard work of researching these stories and tying them together in their episode, "Colors."

Let's start back in the 19th century with a man named William Ewart Gladstone. During his lifetime, he served as British Prime Minister four times—more terms than any other Prime Minister in British history. But in addition to his political work, he was a connoisseur of Homer—you know, the guy whose epic poems you read in middle school–*The Odyssey, The Illiad.*

While writing "Studies on Homer and the Homeric Age," Gladstone began noticing the odd use of color in the poems. Phrases like "wine dark sea" and sections where the author would compare the color of wine to the color of oxen. Gladstone noted Homer's description of lambs having "dark violet wool." He also used violet to describe iron. And he used the color green to describe both honey and "faces pale with fear."

Then Gladstone noticed something else. The color black appears 170 times in the poems. The color white, 100 times. Then there's a dramatic drop off. Red only appears 13 times. Yellow, less than 10 times. Green also less than 10 times. And... wait for it... the color blue never appears in the entirety of either *The Odyssey* or *The Iliad*. This led Gladstone to believe the ancient Greeks were colorblind. In his 1858 book, he wrote, " ... that the organ of color and its impressions were but partially developed among the Greeks of the heroic age".

People mocked him and thought the suggestion the ancient Greeks were colorblind was rather ridiculous. Then, in 1880, Gladstone got further support when a philologist (one who studies ancient texts) by the name of Lazarus Geiger published his findings in "Contributions to the History of the Development of the Human Race." Geiger expounded upon Gladstone's idea by searching through Icelandic sagas, ancient Chinese writings, Indian Vedic hymns and even the Bible. What did he discover? None of these ancient writings mention the color blue. That's right. Even in the Bible, there is no mention of the color blue in the original language.

Geiger wrote,

"These hymns of more than 10k lines are brimming with descriptions of the heavens. Scarcely is there a subject invoked more frequently. The sun and reddening dawn's play of color, day and night, cloud and lightning, the air and the ether are unfolded before us, and over and over its splendor in vivid fullness, but there's only one thing that no one would ever learn from those ancient songs who do not already know it: And that is that the sky is blue."

Nowhere in these Vedic hymns, nor in David's poetic Psalms, or in any of these other books of antiquity across the globe, is a single mention of the color blue. In fact, looking at these works over time, there is a common chronology of the use of color words. They start with black and white. Then the color red is introduced into the language, followed by green and yellow. Blue is always last to appear.

"Hmm," people began to think. "Maybe Gladstone was right. Perhaps this points to an evolutionary change in humanity's ability to actually see color."

Then came Jules Davidoff, Professor of Psychology and Director of the Centre for Cognition, Computation and Culture (CCCC) at Goldsmith's University of London. Regarding his research in the field of color, Davidoff says "working in cultures (Papua New Guinea and Namibia) with minimal colour lexicons, we are studying the effects on the way speakers of the language perceive, categorise and remember colours."

Davidoff and subsequent researches have visited the Himba people of Namibia. In their language, they only have five color words versus our 11 in the English language. Like Homer, they have some interesting descriptions of color. The BBC show, Horizon, followed a researcher doing color cognition studies in the region. In the video, the Himba use their word for "white" to describe milk. But they also use the same word to describe water. Additionally, they use their word for "black" to describe the sky. Next, the researcher shows images with 12 colored squares on them. The first image has a set of green squares. All the squares are the same shade of green except for one square, which is just a slightly different shade of green. The squares are so similar in their shades of green that, to most westerner's eyes, they are impossible to differentiate. But the Himba people are able to recognize the odd one out almost immediately.

Next, the researches show the Himba a second image. This image also has a set of green squares, but one of the squares is a shade of light blue. The contrast is stark. While the difference is most likely immediately obvious to you and me, the Himba people sit for prolonged periods of time, unable to determine which square is blue. Eventually, many give up and make an arbitrary guess. (Additional details on the Himba story sourced from BBC Horizon, "Do You See What I See?")

SPIRITUAL INNOVATION

The language of the people contributed to their ability to see or not see the differentiation of the color.

The same can be true for our limited American English vocabulary. The Himba have several words for cattle which give them a more acute ability to differentiate and categorize them. Popular examples of the nuance of language are the "Eskimo's multiple words for snow" (which isn't actually the case. They have about the same number of words for snow as English) and the multiple words for "love" in the Bible (which is a good example. There are three). When vocabulary is expanded, we have the ability to grasp new concepts and think in new ways.

LANGUAGE AND REALITY

I was talking to my friend Matt about this concept one afternoon, and he said to me, "Oh! Have you heard of Umami?"

"Nope, what's that?" I replied.

You know how you and I grew up with that diagram of a tongue? In elementary school, they taught us, "Sweet, sour, bitter and salty." We did little semi-scientific taste tests to determine which category the unknown foods fit into. And we had 4 options. "For each food, choose "A" for sweet, "B" for sour..." and so on. But all the while there was a fifth option—umami!

Auguste Escoffier was a chef in Paris in the late 1800s. He became famous for his inventive cooking which was derived from his perfection of veal stock, a rich source of the amino acid, glutamate.

Escoffier knew he was onto something, but the science "was discovered in 1908 by Kikunae Ikeda, a Tokyo chemist who identified [the allure of that stock] as the savoury flavour imparted by foods rich in chemicals including glutamate, a building block of protein," writes Heidi Blake in The Telegraph. She goes on to say, "In 2000, researchers at the University of Miami discovered receptors on the tongue that react only to glutamate—suggesting the body craves umami flavours as an indicator of protein in meat and vegetables." (http://www.telegraph.co.uk/foodanddrink/foodanddrinknews/7195114/Umami-in-a-tube-fifth-taste-goes-on-sale-in-supermarkets.html)

But the discovery of umami wasn't just scientifically important. For 2,400 years, humankind lived with an awareness of the four other basic components of taste. Umami had been there all along in foods such as mushrooms, ripe tomatoes, meats and in some cheeses. But with the naming of umami came an intentional highlighting of the flavor. It was no longer just in a meal by accident. There was now an intentionality about the presence of umami in certain dishes. There was a process by which chefs were now searching out sources of umami and including it in their creations. For those in the eating public who are aware of the flavor, there was also a perceptibility for the flavor that brought an added level of acuteness to the eating experience.

"Those who pay careful attention to their tastebuds will discover in the complex flavour of asparagus, tomatoes, cheese and meat, a common and yet absolutely singular taste which cannot be called sweet, or sour, or salty, or bitter..."

- Dr. Kikunae Ikeda, Eighth International Congress of Applied Chemistry, Washington 1912 (http://www.umamiinfo.com/2011/02/the-discovery-of-umami.php)

When I first heard of umami, I thought to myself, "I know exactly what you're talking about." I have always said I like salty foods. But it's not so much salty I like. It's umami. In fact, as I read more about the descriptions of umami, there were times in which the back part of my mouth would tense up a little and begin to salivate, filling my mouth with saliva. For my entire life, I only had the ability to describe my world with the vocabulary and concepts I already knew. All the while, there was this thing below the surface I recognized on a subconscious level. It wasn't until the words were given to me to describe the concept that I suddenly understood it in an entirely different way. This opened me up not only to a deeper level of understanding, but a deeper level of experience as well.

So this can happen for us with senses, like sight (colors) or taste (umami) but can this happen for us spiritually? Is it possible God is busy revealing himself to us with new words and more complex language?

In Acts 19, Paul encounters some disciples from Ephesus and asks them, "Did you receive the Holy Spirit when you believed?"

They respond, "No, we have not even heard that there is a Holy Spirit."

These disciples were disciples of John. Paul goes on to tell them of Jesus, the one about whom John was prophesying. They subsequently are baptized in the name of Jesus. Paul places his hands on them and "The Holy Spirit came on them, and they spoke in tongues and prophesied."

These men had not heard of Jesus, nor had they heard of the Holy Spirit, but by hearing, they were opened up to a new reality. Once opened to this new reality, it not only increased their understanding, it radically shifted their experience. I can't help but wonder if we might be missing important aspects of our experience with God—new facets of our spirituality—because we are closed to new ways of thinking and talking about Him. Can we be curious enough, courageous enough, to gain new language?

LANGUAGE AND INNOVATION

What's amazing to me is the realization that every word ever spoken was used for the first time at one point. There was a time in which the word, and therefore the concept of, "I" was spoken into existence for the first time. Perhaps there was a level of self-awareness before the uttering of the word, maybe even some level of selfishness. But the introduction of the word "I" changed our ability to perceive our own selves—our own existence. It brought definition to our individuality. It increased our level of awareness of an individual's separation from everything and everyone around it.

In the same way, we have words like "love" and "peace"—huge realities that we are able to grasp (or at least begin to grasp) thanks to language. Each of us has felt the depths of love and its many facets. We've sensed moments of peace and serenity. Which leads me to ask: could there be things as real as love and peace that we've yet to uncover because we are not yet able to name them? Perhaps there are parts of the human experience we experience intuitively or subconsciously, but we haven't actually experienced their depth and meaning because we haven't identified them yet. If the people of ages past would have said, "surely not," perhaps we wouldn't even know of love or peace. Like umami, we might sense something there, just below the surface, but being able to name it allows us to step into a more full realization and outliving of it.

This idea came one night in worship. Our regular worship gathering was over, but there were still things happening. I said, "if you want to stay a bit longer and worship, we'll do it." There might have been about 100 people remaining in the room. My friend Ryan was leading musically that night. As we continued to lead together, he looked over at me and said something that has stuck with me for a couple years.

SPIRITUAL INNOVATION

"God is going to do things we won't even have words for. We're going to have to be part of creating a new vocabulary."

Lander later reinforced that same idea by saying: "You're going to move from reading about things you've never seen into a place of seeing things you've never read about."

Even in writing this book I've experienced that to be true. For me, the title, "Spiritual Innovation," has significant meaning. As I've been on this journey, the phrase has helped me see things in a different light. It's helped me discover things about God and His truth that would have previously been hidden. Thinking about my relationship with God in terms of innovation has helped me remain in a posture of celebrating that God has been moving, is moving and will continue to move in ways that exceed my expectation. I hope the term itself will help bring a new layer to the Christian conversation. I hope and pray it will be something that helps us think about and experience our life with God in a new way.

SHIFTING ENVIRONMENTS

I was at the airport soon after the 2013 Boston Marathon. Traditionally, this would have been a time of celebration and victory—a time of personal accomplishment for about 27,000 runners from all over the world. But this year's event was marked by two explosions, near the finish line, about four hours after the start of the race. Two days after the explosion, I was in the airport.

The computer system of the airline I was flying had gone down and hundreds of flights had been grounded for over two hours. There were thousands of people packed into the airport waiting for the system to come back up. I decided to charge my phone at a charging station. It was an island in the middle of the airport, around which about a dozen other travelers had gathered.

A young attractive couple came over. The wife, I think her name was Kate, pulled out her phone and charger and shared the other plug in my outlet. I noticed she was wearing a Boston Marathon jacket. She began telling me and the others within earshot about her experience. Despite the tragic event, she had finished the race. We were smiling and celebrating her victory together. It was a reminder of all the successes that had occurred that day, despite the tragedy.

An older man with a red face edged his way over to the charging station. He had been sitting in a chair on the outskirts of the island, but the conversation had piqued his interest, so he approached. He looked at Kate with a scowl and a furrowed brow and, in a gruff voice commanded, "You better thank God you weren't hurt." He went on to talk about how bad he saw the world getting and how the way we lived was about to change for the worse. As he was talking, I thought to myself, "You know, I bet his experience with the world is as bad as he thinks the rest of the world is." We had been having a conversation that acknowledged a senseless, horrible, anomaly of an event; but that ultimately celebrated the accomplishment of this young woman. The tenor of the conversation was celebration and congratulations. We were smiling. We were happy for her. And yet when this man entered into the environment, the atmosphere shifted. His words and his demeanor shifted the reality for all of us.

This experience made me wonder: "What's the difference between a non-Christian who detonates a bomb and a Christian who declares and hopes for destruction on the earth?" Scripture says that "The power of life and death is in the tongue." If the enemy can convince those with powerful speech to proclaim curses over the earth, he has a powerful ally in his agenda of destruction. A terrorist can plant a bomb and bring temporary fear by external means. But a Christian can speak in alignment with the spiritual realm and bring spiritual realities into existence. There is power in our blessing and there is power in our cursing. We must be careful with our words.

Earlier that afternoon, as I sat on the cold, hard tile of the airport, waiting for news on my delayed flight, I started to feel a spirit of complaining rise up in me. I was uncomfortable. I was packed into the airport with thousands of other upset travelers. All the seats were taken. Everything in me wanted someone to pay. I gathered my things, stood up and started to walk. Blessing or cursing? I knew I had a conscious choice to make. I could walk around pointing out the (relative) misery of our situation. I could complain to a gate agent. I could be upset that someone, somewhere should be working faster to resolve the problem. But on this occasion, I chose blessing. "Lord, bless the thousands of people sitting in this airport right now. Bless the gate agents who are trying to make the best of a bad situation. Even bless the people working to solve the problem in some server room in some distant place." I was picturing a guy with glasses working on some code somewhere, fixing the bug in a system, or some hardware problem that had rendered the system inoperable. In that moment, he was relaxing. The shaking of his hands was slowing. His breathing was becoming more regular. His mind was becoming more clear. And, without pressure, he was resolving the problem more quickly and peacefully.

Without a doubt, I know my shift in attitude and thinking affected the spiritual realm. Even if in a very small way, it shifted the spiritual temperature of that airport terminal and the room where that problem was being solved. Can you imagine what would happen if there were dozens of people—or hundreds of people—in that airport terminal choosing to shift the spiritual reality? All I can think is: kingdom of heaven.

Cursing or blessing? Death or life? Everything we say has the power to bring one or the other. You and I have been entrusted with a great power in such a small vessel. We have the ability to thwart evil and bring life through the simplicity of our words. That is Spiritual Innovation and it impacts more than just your own private spiritual life—it radiates and impacts the entire world around you.

Our words are continually revealing something, inviting something, and creating something. What will it be?

QUESTIONS AND CONVERSATIONS :

- Do you think words affect the world around you? How? Are there certain words you use or don't use for a specific reason? What are those reasons?

- How have you seen the language you use or do not use affect your surroundings or a situation? Perhaps it's how you responded to something someone else said. Perhaps it's something you spoke proactively in a moment. How have you seen your words shape your surroundings?

- Remember a time you heard a word for the first time. Did it have an effect on that moment or a moment since you learned the word? What do you think about the idea that there are concepts similar to "peace" that have yet to be identified and named?

DO SOMETHING :

Look for a thing or concept this week that you perceive, sense or experience that may not have a name. If you think there might be a name for that thing, research it. See how naming it can shift how you interact with or perceive that thing. Share the word and concept with someone else.

SPIRITUAL INNOVATION // CHAPTER ELEVEN
PERMISSION TO CREATE

SPIRITUAL INNOVATION

You and I love to have control—control of our own lives, control of situations, control of environments, control over other people. We, as humans, love being in control. And yet our need for control will always keep us from revelation, from Spiritual Innovation.

If there's one thing that has been instrumental in teaching me how to let go of control, it's creativity.

Early in my life, the expression of creativity was quite controlled. I grew up singing in church—and most of the singing done in church is singing other people's songs. I was thankful for the things God did through those songs. I was thankful for how convenient it was to look at lyrics sheets and chord charts and just play someone else's song. Like many other areas of my faith, it was easier to believe God would give that stuff to someone else, in another time an another place. It was easier to believe God spoke to other people through songs, but not to me, not in that way.

But there came a time when I knew there was something more to being a musician. I sensed there was something stirring, and to be responsible with that stirring meant writing songs. I had no context for writing songs. I had no environment in which I was encouraged to write. There wasn't anyone in my immediate vicinity to look up to or to learn from. And being out there all alone made me feel really vulnerable.

THE CREATIVE PROCESS

Creating something—whether a song or a painting or a sculpture or even writing a book—is a nebulous, indescribable process, but it's important for us to talk about what it takes to be creative because creativity teaches us about life and faith. Sure there are lots of books and teachers who talk about "how to be creative." But really, there's something to creating that's beyond the realm of teaching. Certain environments can help you hone your skills or provide an outlet for creating consistently, but the da Vinci's, Dali's, Dillion's, and Depp's of our world aren't solely the product of education. They're people who were able to tap into something unseen, something beyond themselves. That's where the creative process starts.

1. Access the Unseen

There's an acting method developed by Japanese director, Tadashi Suzuki that recognizes what Suzuki calls, "satz." This is the moment before the action or movement of the actor in which he or she decides how to move. It's not an intellectual decision. It involves listening deeply, internally, and responding as led. This is one example of accessing that unknown, deep place in the creative process. It's about overcoming the constant human propensity to guard ourselves and search for safety by filtering our decisions through our perceptions of the expected responses of others. Satz, on the other hand, is about making a choice, not by filtering but by responding in the moment to a deeply internal prompt. Satz is a perfect example of accessing the unseen in the creative process.

Once an artist has opened themselves up to the unseen component of creativity and has an idea, we come to the next step.

2. Bring the idea into existence.

After we have an idea, artists begin working to bring that idea from the unseen realm into the realm of the senses. The work of creating art is about taking a piece of inspiration and making it manifest in a way in which others can encounter it.

I experienced this in working on a sculpture project with my friend, Josh. He wanted to explore light and the power of bringing things from a hidden place into the light of honesty. I wanted to explore one of the constant themes of my life: relationship and connectivity—the reality that we are exponentially more effective together than we are alone. So, together, we began asking, "How do we manifest these themes? How do we bring them from the realm of ideas and into the realm of the senses?" From that, we created the Tree of Light, a 20-foot tall, 20-foot diameter sculpture of a tree. It's made with an aluminum skeleton and covered with recycled and reclaimed wood. From the tree's seven branches hang 40 light bulbs with pull strings. Patrons pull the strings to turn on the lights. Once all the lights are on, the bulbs "dance" through a programed sequence to an original piece of music, and then return to black to start all over again. Through this piece, we realized we had the ability to help people experience, firsthand, the themes that previously only existed existentially.

The next part in the creative process is the most difficult for me:

3. Present the work to the rest of humanity.

There's a whole new level of vulnerability in moving from that guy who just plays and sings in his bedroom—to the artist who presents his work to the world. What's the first question we've learned to ask when walking out of a movie theater? "Did you like it?" The primary expectation we have of one another in encountering a creative work is not that we would be moved or changed or affected. The primary expectation we have of one another in encountering a creative work is judgement. "Did you like it?" Personally, I've stopped answering (and asking) the question. My response is usually, "Does it matter?" Some things are crucially important or life changing—and yet I hate them. Some things I "like" are inconsequential. We mustn't allow our fear of inevitable judgement ("do you like it?") of our creative work stop us from unveiling that work to the world.

After these three steps in the process—accessing the unseen, manifesting the work, and presenting it to the world—we come to the last step:

4. The work affects the world.

People have a response. Even more importantly, we've contributed something meaningful to the human conversation. We've shared our own revelation. We've reflected the qualities and character of God to our community in a unique way.

The reason I outline this process in the context of this book is because there is little difference between the creative process and the Christian process. In our desire for control, artists and Christians alike want to *learn* ourselves into growth. We want to "learn" to become a better artist or a "better Christian." Of course, like art, the Christian life involves honing gifts through practice and refinement of skill, but there has to be a different seed, a deeper starting place. We start by accessing the unseen—the Holy Spirit. Once we've experienced that deep place with the Lord, we step into the next part—bringing spiritual realities into physical existence—the kingdom of heaven or the fruit of the Spirit or the message of Christ through word or deed. Next, we present that thing to the world. Lastly, there is a response.

When we create art we have the opportunity to say something to the world. And when we live a life of supernatural power we say, "Spiritual Innovation is real and possible." You can be uniquely you and still a believer. You don't have to copy those who have come before you (myself included). God is busy revealing himself to you in a brand new way.

We can't do the Christian life—can't bring the kingdom of heaven to earth or tell people about the love God has for them—without creativity, without innovation.

SPIRITUAL INNOVATION

"I'M NOT CREATIVE"

I often hear people declare themselves, "not creative." In saying so, they mean, "I don't paint" or "I can't sing" or "don't ask me to get in front of people and talk." So, let's come to a more broad, working understanding of creativity.

We often talk about God as Creator. There's a recognition that one of the characteristics of God and the image He's placed in us is His identity as Creator. It seems to me this is one of those concepts we only recognize as a nice idea, but don't see as an embodiment for the whole of the Christian life. We use it to give validity to our paintings and our songs—which is good. But I believe there's something deeper to the image of the Creator, beyond poetry, art, and music that lies within each of us.

Creativity, in the Christian sense, is not about painting pictures of crosses or footprints in the sand or nice landscapes. It's about something much larger. It is an integral part of what it means to be a Christian—to be *incarnational*. We are commissioned to access the heart of God and manifest His realities in the lives and circumstances around us. That's creativity. That's innovation.

Instead, we've reduced the power of creativity and replaced it with art that is "nice." When we paint a cross, we cheat. For years, I traveled with some of my best friends playing music. We would often lead worship musically at camps and retreats. One of the camps we played at had hired an artist to come do live painting. He started with a large, blank canvas. The audio tech pressed play, and as the "christian music" montage began, he would dip his hands into various buckets and begin to paint. This night, his pallet consisted of the colors of a sunset. He painted the orange sky, some brown, rolling hills, and a large sun toward the top of the canvas—all this in about 3 minutes. It was pretty impressive. Then he dipped his hand in some black paint and began painting a path through the rolling hills and off into the distance. From my perspective, it was a fairly clear message: "We're all on a journey in life. We have ups and downs, but there's always a path to follow." After six or seven minutes of painting, the last song of the montage was winding down. The painter dipped his index finger in a small cup of white paint and there, at the top of the hill, at the end of the path through the mountains, he placed three small, white crosses. And suddenly, the painting became "Christian."

What's ironic about using the cross to give us a sense that a painting is "Christian?" The cross is about pain. It's about suffering. It's about hard work and figuring out and working through and not knowing. And we strip it of its meaning by making it the cherry on top of our art work. Rather than making a piece of art which invites people into a moment of reflection or introspection or conflict or emotional response, we make the art easy for the consumer. If it has a cross or a fish or Jesus or a lamb or a (curved) rainbow, then it's Christian. It can be hung in a church office or a good Christian home. If any of these tell-tale signs are not apparent in the work, it has not been pre-approved by the Christian industrial machine for safe consumption by the masses. Beware.

True creativity is not this clean, this easy—neither is truly, authentically, living a life with Christ.

And yet we've done the same things with our church buildings, our music, our sermons, our church gatherings, and our Christian lives. If they have the cultural signposts of what it means to be "Christian" in our culture, then they fit into our "spiritual" box. If not, they are threatening or frivolous and, therefore, dismissed.

Sure, Jesus plainly said exactly what he meant sometimes. But more often than not, people walked away from their conversations with Jesus wondering. Creativity does something exposition cannot. It is a delivery method like no other. That's one of the beautiful things about Jesus' use of parables. While our era wants to satisfy intellectual curiosity by providing satisfying answers to life's questions, Jesus responded to questions with stories. He didn't answer in a way that people would walk away satisfied. Rather, he told stories that resulted with people coming back to him with more questions. Isn't that interesting? The stories Jesus told caused people to keep asking more and deeper questions, which led them deeper into relationship with Him.

He certainly didn't make the "A" list when it came to the external, cultural indicators of what it meant to be a first century Jew. And yet, rather than spending his time fulfilling other's expectations of him, he gave his time and energy to creating a whole new world (don't you dare close your eyes). That's what it means to be creative. That is Spiritual Innovation.

That's what it would really look like to live like Jesus.

Creativity, in the Christian sense, is about manifesting the fruits of the Spirit in situations where it might seem impossible. It's about manifesting love in an environment that is love-less. It's about manifesting peace in the midst of chaos. It's about overcoming depression with joy, hate with kindness, evil with goodness, hostility with gentleness. That's what it means to be creative, to be innovative, to be Christ-like. I don't know about you, but that's something I can get behind.

LOSING CONTROL

Growing up around theme parks has made me used to guard rails. When you have tens of thousands of children running around a place, barriers can be a good thing. And yet the first time I visited the Grand Canyon, I was blown away. Not a single guard rail anywhere. Just cliffs with thousand-foot falls to certain death. Part of me has to wonder what it would be like to just jump.

I admit: I'm a tiny bit of a dare devil. I have a crazy urge inside me that—whenever I pass by a police officer—I like to imagine how I could get his gun before he could taze me or billy club me or whatever his defensive tactic would be. The Grand Canyon is not a great place for people with insane impulses like the one I've just confessed and yet, up until this point, thankfully, I've exhibited enough self-control to *not* test my ninja-like reflexes on the police officer in line at the deli—or to walk off the edge of the Grand Canyon. Both of these impulses remind me of the deep desire implanted in each one of us to buck safety and try to fly off the edge of a cliff.

There's an improv game called Blind Freeze. It goes like this: the actors line up at the back of the stage. Two players step out and improvise a scene while one of the other players has his back to the scene. At some point, one of the actors from the ensemble will yell "freeze". The improvisors in the scene freeze in their positions. The player with his back to the scene turns around, tags one of the frozen players out and then starts a whole new scene based on those positions.

We played this game in a class I taught called "Be Present: The intersection of faith and the arts." It's based on what the principles of acting and improvisation teach us about our relationship with God. It has been amazing to see the transformation of the actors in the class through something as simple as Blind Freeze. To the observer, Blind Freeze might seem like a simple game of non-sense. Depending on the eyes of the viewer and/or participant, it can seem frivolous. But, like most art, there is something much deeper going on below the surface.

At first, I just told the actors in the class "how" to play the game. I explained it to them as I have explained it in the previous paragraph. As we'd play, one of the ensemble members would yell, "freeze."

SPIRITUAL INNOVATION

The "blind" player would turn around and slowly approach the two players in the scene—examining them as if they were relics from ancient Greece. You could see, behind their eyes, the synapses firing. "What can I do with this?" "What will be funny?" "If I choose that, the others might think I'm stupid." "No, I'm not going to start that scene." "Even I think that's stupid." "Eh, I guess I'll settle on this."

Do you see what happened? There was a constant process of editing in an attempt to minimize risk and the effects of unintended consequences. Just like our everyday lives, these actors were trying to "figure it out." They were reinforcing the human habit of leaning on our own understanding in hopes of not doing anything *too* foolish. Dr Charles Limb, in his 2012 TED Talk showed new research in the area of jazz improvisation and the brain. While the research is preliminary, he noted that during improvisation, "we have this combination of an area [of the brain] that's thought to be involved in self-monitoring turning off, and this area that's thought to be autobiographical or self-expressive turning on." He goes on to say, "to be creative you have to have this weird dissociation in your frontal lobe. One area turns on, and a big area shuts off so that you're not inhibited so that you're willing to make mistakes so that you're not constantly shutting down all these new, generative impulses."

84% of children rank high in creativity in Kindergarten

10% rank high in creativity in grade 2

What happens to us between those two short years of age five and age seven?

In just two years of modern, western education, children are conditioned *out* of the belief they can fly and into a world of guard rails. They are taught to do the assignment "correctly." They are conditioned to conform to expectations. They are shamed into social boxes, stigmas, and structures. And thus begins the constant process of living an edited—a controlled—life.

But an edited life is the antithesis of art, creativity, and innovation. The stories we want to see and hear unfolded before us on stage, on screen, in a song, a sculpture, or a painting are the stories of the lives we really want to be *living*. The stories we admire lived out in front of us are the ones that don't value safety as their first priority. Art is a vehicle that reminds us of who we're really meant to be.

As the actors continued playing Blind Freeze, I encouraged them with this: "Stop walking slowly in an attempt to give yourself more time to figure things out. Get to the scene. Tap one of the actors out. Take the position, and in taking on the position, you'll know who you are. The scene will come from that."

There's a small taco place north of downtown Orlando in the Mills/50 District called Tako Cheena. My friend Jake loves the place, and we walk there frequently. It's one of those "open late" kind of places but serves something better than diner food. There are always bikes locked up out front and they keep the door open and the air conditioner off far too long into spring. So the patrons enjoy their late night tacos under a sheen of sweat—born from spice, heat, and humidity. It's probably not the best conditions for art, but they always have a rotating selection on the walls. This night, Jake and I were each so drawn to separate pieces of art, we ended up adding them both to our purchases that night.

At first I was just intrigued by a texturized oil-on-canvas painting. It had two figures on it: one of them a rabbit, the other some sort of pop-art, comical creature. The rabbit had a look of terror. He was obviously uncomfortable because of something outside the window of the painting. The other character was looking partly at the rabbit and partly out into our world. Above the comical creature was a speech bubble with the words, "ad lib" in them. I was drawn in by the scene and the emotion of these two characters, but I wasn't quite sold. Maybe the art wasn't timely enough. Perhaps it would look passé—the work of a bygone era—a decade from now. But then, I saw the title: The Show Must Go On. That, I knew, was a timeless message—as was the look of terror on that rabbit's face and the "ad lib" coming out of the mouth of his friend. I bought it and it now hangs on our wall at home.

The way I see it, the painting captures the danger of the creative life. It recognizes and embraces the unknown nature of stepping out in risk. The painting captures the moment of those performers in Blind Freeze stepping out, taking a position and starting a scene. It embodies risk of writing a song and playing it for a room full of people. It reflects the invigorating moment of telling someone you love them for the first time. And it celebrates the beauty of a life with God—full of discovering and the unknown and meaning.

Creativity and safety are incompatible.

Creativity is willing to step into the unknown and bring something new into existence. Creativity is about an unbridled, unstoppable heart.

And so is life with God.

What are you waiting for?

DOORSTEP DELIVERY

For a long time, growing up in church, I thought my creative pursuits were separate from God. I sensed they were considered by many to be unwieldily and frivolous. I remember beginning to explore some creative ways to worship and engage God beyond the typical music and teaching of my youth. One of the pastors of the church I was part of at the time began asking questions, "What exactly is it you guys are doing over there? Why are you lighting candles? And what did you do with that magna-doodle? Some people are coming to me, asking questions. They're a little worried about what you're getting into."

This event—the fact that this pastor felt he had to check in on me—was about safety and control, and more than ever it made it clear to me that creativity and safety were incompatible.

So is life with God.

Art isn't only *about* life. It's practice *for* life.

It was at this point in my life I began to see creativity is not only practice for life with God. Creativity can also be a conduit between the natural and the supernatural, the temporal and the eternal, the seen and the unseen. In other words, creativity delivers the divine into the world and helps the world transcend into the divine. It's about bringing heaven to earth.

This is one of the reasons I love leading worship musically so much. Over time, God has developed in me the ability to sense His presence and movement in a gathering of people and cultivate it. There are lots of philosophies about the role of music in the church. There's the idea that it's there to set up the message (gag). Some would say it's to teach theology in the form of a song (sure, that can be helpful). But music isn't solely cognitive. Nor is it simply emotional. Music has the ability to create deeply spiritual moments.

In 2 Kings, Elisha is asked by the king to deliver a word from the Lord. Elisha's first request was "now bring me a harpist" and then "while the harpist was playing, the hand of the Lord came on Elisha." The music became a supernatural delivery system. The same thing happened when David was called into the King Saul's chamber. "Whenever the spirit from God came on Saul, David would take up his lyre and play. Then relief would come to Saul; he would feel better, and the evil spirit would leave him." What a beautiful testimony to the power of creativity.

The modern worship movement has been so powerful because, somehow, it has stumbled back into this deep reality of the power of music to be a conduit between the natural and supernatural. There were people who believed, "Surely there must be more to the role of music in the church. There must be another way, other than standing up on stage singing *at* people, waving our hands to the beat. There must be some way to innovate in this area." And as they risked, they started writing songs and creating environments in which people were connecting deeply with God.

But the deep connection we've seen and experienced with God through music is just the beginning.

Before stepping into the pastor position at City Beautiful Church, I was the Creative Director for four years. I started doing the things I thought a Creative Director should do—music, graphics, an occasional video. But I quickly became restless in the limited scope of those duties. "There has to be something more," I thought to myself. Eventually, I realized I wanted to move from the presentational to the invitational. I recognized art as a supernaturally powerful force which connects deeply in the spirits of those who are willing. Fortunately, I was in a church community of risk-takers who trusted one another and would step into the unknown quite willingly. It was a perfect incubator.

So, we embarked on a journey into the experiential. I began asking, "How can we move from telling people about spiritual ideas into experiencing them first hand? How can we not only make art *about* life? How can we allow art to be practice *for* life?"

One night, we were investigating the spiritual reality of faith. "Okay, how do we create an experience that helps us illuminate and experience faith?" At the end of the message, we invited people to write on an index card an area of their lives in which they desired a greater level of faith. Our main auditorium held about 700, and next to that was a smaller room. We decided to black out the smaller room, and using stanchions and rope, we created a path through the room. "The rope starts here in the middle of the main room. In one hand, hold the index card. With the other hand, take the rope, and allow it to lead you through the dark room next door. As you walk, pray for an increase of faith in the area of your life you wrote on the index card."

It was amazing to see people walking by faith—literally. Then to hear them talk about their experience afterward. "I actually had a hard time praying because I was afraid I would run into someone by going too fast. Or that I would hold everyone up by going too slow." Another person said, "I just closed my eyes and went for it. I knew I couldn't see anyway, so I just trusted that the rope wasn't going to trick me. Once I let go of my fears, I could just trust."

So much more is possible when we let go of our fears and learn to trust.

This is just one of hundreds of experiences we cultivated when we began exploring. Eventually, a few friends and I began to see how art was a conduit for divine connection —both inside and outside the church. Three friends (John David, Holly, Aradhana) and I began working on an interactive theater experience, called "Connected," about the things that cause us to connect and disconnect from one another relationally. We debuted it as part of an international theater festival in Orlando. The show followed one character—Jacob—as he encountered several moments from his past that wounded him and caused him to disconnect from the people around him. As he re-encountered these moments, he was able to heal from them and reengage more deeply with the people in his current day context.

SPIRITUAL INNOVATION

We wired every seat in the theater with a set of earbuds through which the audience members were directed by "The Guide" through several introspective moments. They were asked to consider their own experiences in light of the story unfolding before them on stage. As the show progressed, the audience participants were asked to become increasingly vulnerable, culminating in a moment in which they wrote on a piece of paper the conclusion to the statement: "Something I wish I had never heard spoken over me is..." There were some beautiful moments of confession in that theater. One individual wrote: "Something I wish I had never heard spoken over me was: 'I wish I had aborted you.'" After the show that night, that theatergoer sought me out and said, "My mother said that to me when I was a boy. It's stuck with me for over 30 years. I'm just now coming to the place of being able to talk about it. Tonight was a huge step for me."

Had we gathered a theater full of people and just asked them to access the deep places of themselves and their past, we most likely would have experienced much resistance. But there was something about the story unfolding before them that gave people permission to be honest and vulnerable. The story of Jacob and the environment we created in that theater connected to a deeply spiritual place inside the audience members. As a result, people opened up.

After the first night of performances at the Orlando International Fringe Theater Festival, one of the cast members came up to me and said, "I was spending time with the Lord this morning, and I heard Him say, 'People are going to experience me through "Connected." They may not know it's me right away, but they'll encounter me again later and think back to their experience in this theater. They'll be willing to engage with me because they got acquainted with me through Connected.'"

To me, this sounds like God and what I know of him. It's what fuels me to keep taking risks, to keep being creative, to push for even more Spiritual Innovation.

Creativity not only teaches us how to take risks and be present and manifest the unseen. Creativity is a delivery method. When talking to worship leaders, I often talk about the worship set as a bed in which people can intimately encounter God. In the midst of the songs, music, and lyrics, we're supernaturally creating a space for intimacy. My role as a worship leader is to see where God is and see where the people are and help them rendezvous somewhere in this sacred space. It's perhaps a crude metaphor—but not because the sexual connotation is too much. Because it is too limited. There is no encounter more intimate than that sacred encounter we, as humans, have with God in the spiritual realm. And creativity is a bridge between those two realms. We experience it in a song. We sense it in a story. We see it in a film. Someone creates something and, mysteriously, God meets us in it.

Again, creativity isn't just *about* our life with God. It *is* our life with God. As we learn to be more creative, more innovative, we learn to experience and manifest more of Him.

When David played that harp in the presence of Saul, there was divine rest in it. God gave David a divinely powerful creativity. Creativity is a conduit through which God meets people and by which people transcend the physical and encounter the divine.

We see this same divine artistry in Exodus 31. God gave Moses instructions for the construction of the tabernacle—specific instructions, which required much skill. Then, in Exodus 31, God says to Moses, "See, I have chosen Bezalel, son of Uri, the son of Hur, of the tribe of Judah, and I have filled him with the Spirit of God, with wisdom, with understanding, with knowledge and with all kinds of skills—to make artistic designs for work in gold, silver and bronze, to cut and set stones, to work in wood, and to engage in all kinds of crafts." (Eric Johnson has an amazing message on this and other passages titled "Ask For Wisdom": Bethel Church, April 14, 2013). This passage is the first mention in all of scripture of someone being filled with the Spirit of God—and it was for the purpose of *empowering* Bezalel creatively so that God could come and dwell with His people.

When we consider the broad understanding of creativity in the Christian life, we see God gives us the ability to dream and operate creatively so He can dwell on the earth. In fact, the problems we encounter in our lives on this earth cease to be an annoyance (like my long wait at the Boston airport) and suddenly become an opportunity for Christians to exhibit divine creativity so the Holy Spirit might dwell in those circumstances and manifest the fruit of His being.

Does this change the way you think about the role of a Christian in this world? I don't know about you, but it has changed everything for me.

There is nothing small or insignificant to God about promoting His kingdom agenda. And since our creative thinking is the means by which he is doing just that, there is nothing small or insignificant about our ability to practice and enact our creativity. He is "able to do immeasurably more than all we ask or imagine, according to his power that is at work within us." This is only the beginning.

God's power at work through the creativity of the Church sets us on the path of asking: "What next, Lord?" and expecting to see it come to be.

QUESTIONS AND CONVERSATIONS :

- Do you consider yourself to be a creative person? How does this affect the way you see and live your faith?

- How do you embody creativity? How are you contributing creatively to the environments you find yourself-at home, at work, at church, socially or civically?

- As you commune with God in the unseen spiritual realm, are there things He's revealing to you so that you can bring those things into existence? Has that happened in the past? How is it happening in your life now? How can you step into a deeper expression of creativity in your faith?

DO SOMETHING :

Make something. Regardless of whether you consider yourself an artist, make something. In fact, if you consider yourself an artist, it may be helpful to make something in a discipline other than the one you usually create in. Pay specific attention to the steps of the creative process :

1. Access the unseen.

2. Bring the idea into existence.

3. Present the work to the rest of humanity.

4. The work affects the world.

As you experience these steps in creating, consider how they parallel your spiritual life.

SPIRITUAL INNOVATION // CHAPTER TWELVE
THE KINGDOM COMES

We've talked about a lot of philosophy and theology. We've discussed the ideas of the kingdom of heaven and God's intentions to bring heaven to earth. But all of this is completely useless if all we do is talk. The goal of this book is not only to get you to see a different reality but also to recognize your role in bringing that reality into existence.

Without this piece, I'm afraid I haven't done this topic justice.

We often talk about changing the world, and when we do, we imagine something distant from our own time, place, and realm of responsibility. But change happens when you and I move from good philosophy to good practice. In Matthew 20, Jesus tells the disciples that "the first shall be last and the last shall be first." He points out the power of servanthood. Then, in the very next passage, Jesus diverts from his journey into Jerusalem to heal two blind men. Jesus changed the world because he did more than preach. He acted.

So how do we step into practical manifestation of these realities?

THE KINGDOM IN YOUR LIFE

We so often want to change the world by looking at other people and asking, "How should their lives be different?" And yet, while being considerate of the needs of others is important, in order to truly bring about the kingdom, it has to start in the life of you and me.

This isn't the way we've been conditioned to think about our spiritual life—that the coming of heaven to earth begins with personal, spiritual pursuit. We've been conditioned to think that pastors, priests or even the Pope has a corner on the market of Truth and we're just supposed to mimic and keep up. But Spiritual Innovation, at it's core, suggests the very opposite: we will be effective in living out Spiritual Innovation when and only when we've chosen to pursue God like never before—when we're asking for Him to accomplish something we haven't seen in the history of humanity, something beyond our good ideas. In order to live this out in real life, we must personally access the unseen heart of God and operate in supernatural wisdom.

No one can live your spiritual life for you. Relationship is the one thing you cannot outsource. That's what the Israelites did by handing off the work of God to the priests. That's what so much of the Evangelical Church has done by elevating pastors to the place of priest and saying, "You go see what God has to say, and come back and tell us what He said."

But the coming of the kingdom in power doesn't begin with an organizational movement. It begins with a multitude of individuals growing ever closer to the heart of God. It means getting into secret places with Him and learning what His voice sounds like. It means knowing what He's said in the past and listening to what He's saying today.

Intimacy with God is born on the altar of sacrifice. It comes from giving our lives, passions, time, and dreams over to a God who wants to exceed what we are able to accomplish on our own. No one else can accomplish what *you've* been created to accomplish in the way *you've* been created to accomplish it. And stepping into the fullness of your calling flows from a continual increase of intimacy with God.

Can you imagine how your life would change if you were willing to admit—and live in— this reality?

God so desperately longs to heal the world through you, and when we step into a new level of commitment to pursuing God with all our heart, mind, soul, and strength, we'll be blown away by how He exceeds our biggest expectations.

SPIRITUAL INNOVATION

This book paints a lot of grandiose pictures, but I can assure you, the pictures painted here pale in comparison to what God can accomplish through a surrendered people full of expectation, creativity, and the spirit of discovery.

THE KINGDOM IN THE CHURCH

In the introduction to this book, I talked about the need to approach the content here with hope, not cynicism. I've hit the Church pretty hard at times and it would be really easy for us to just give up on the Church altogether. But you and I aren't meant to accomplish this work alone. It's not enough to just pursue God on your own. It's not enough to have a private faith.

The work of the kingdom is a collaborative effort.

God could have done all this work on His own. Christ could have snapped his fingers and brought the fullness of the kingdom of heaven through the veil of invisibility and into the seen realm in an instant. God could have had everything come through you and your personal, private faith. But none of those things are the case. For whatever reason, God has chosen to invite you and me—in relationship together—into the work of reconciling the entire universe back to Himself.

Right now, the Church exists in an extreme level of division and disunity, but that can change within your lifetime. Right now, we see almost comical excuses for division: drums in the sanctuary, the color of the carpet or pews, predestination versus free will. The religious spirit has been at work for centuries—knowing that the more the church is divided, the less effective it will be in accomplishing that which God has commissioned us into.

The longer we focus on the division, the more distracted we will become from Spiritual Innovation.

DIVIDED WE FALL

For 15 centuries, the church was just that—THE church. There was only one church, "the holy catholic church" as the Apostle's Creed puts it. Growing up, I just thought that "catholic" word referred to the body of people belonging to Roman Catholicism. But in this case, it's small "c" catholic, meaning "including a wide variety of things; all-embracing."

At the beginning of 2013, I was at our church's mid week prayer gathering. It was in that time I heard in my spirit a phrase I had never even considered before. "During your lifetime, you can see the end of denominational division." It wasn't a statement of what "will" be but what "could" be. It's a statement of possibility—seeing the kingdom come in power because we, His Church, have been willing to lay down our pride, our walls and our stubbornness and step into a unity not seen in the Church for almost 2000 years.

Then, another word. This one even more unbelievable to my natural mind, "You could even see an end to the Catholic/Protestant divide around the world." I began to cry. It was a glimpse of the kingdom truly come to earth. It was a unified Church, living as its meant to live.

But, the Church today has a lot of history to redeem in the process.

While there had been minor defections from the Church over the 1500 years of its existence, Martin Luther's defection was the second major schism that created such an exodus from that initial unified body. (The first being the East-West Schism of 1054 creating the Eastern and Western/Roman Catholic divisions. And even in this division, there was only one split—as opposed to the ongoing

SPIRITUAL INNOVATION

division resulting from the Protestant Reformation.) And this Protestant Reformation was the foundation upon which the denominational Church was built. As a result, we have seen a continued breakdown of God's intention for a unified Church.

The Protestant Reformation was the beginning of a mass exodus from Roman Catholicism. Of course, there were benefits that flowed from the Reformation. It re-empowered followers of Christ to actively engage with Him without the need for an earthly priest. It set the Church on the course of a greater understanding of justification by faith. But, it was built upon the concept of protest—a protest against the selling of indulgences and the unjust treatment of laity, primarily. These were important issues and should have been addressed. But how they were addressed was the beginning of a continual expectation of division based on disagreement. As a result, splits continued to occur around decreasingly less important doctrinal interpretations—and worse.

As time progressed, divisions continued. Denominational "leadership" cemented the example of organizational defection in the hearts and minds of people. And what began as organizational sin was soon adopted into the daily lives of congregants.

That leads us to today. Often we chuckle about church splits that have occurred over things as silly as the color of carpet in the building. We reduce it to people being petty. Or we accept as normal the tendency of people to hop from one church to another hoping to be "fed." But I am increasingly convinced that issues like these are the fruit of seeds that have been growing out of the Protestant Defection for the last 500 years. This defection, an epic and grave event, 500 years ago, is now the everyday norm of millions of Christians all over the world on a continual basis.

So does it even matter? Absolutely yes.

As a result of the increase of denominational division, we now take refuge in bastions of cookie-cutter interpretation. We come out of our homogeneous silos only to confront one another in debate at the doors of the Castle Church of Wittenberg all over again. We write scathing blog posts and magazine articles. We miss great implications to our own spiritual lives by categorically dismissing interpretations, experiences or even entire passages of scripture as the realm of "the Calvinists" or "the Pentecostals" or "the Baptists." And because we've done so well at surrounding ourselves with those who think and act just like us, we're never confronted with the iron-sharpening discomfort of "different."

In Galatians 5, we see a list of attributes that are common to those "who will not inherit the kingdom of God."

"...sexual immorality, impurity and debauchery; idolatry and witchcraft; hatred, discord, jealousy, fits of rage, selfish ambition, dissensions, factions and envy; drunkenness, orgies, and the like." (Galatians 5:19-21)

The Church is really great at flashing this verse in the eyes of the "sexually immoral" and "idolators." But right there, in the middle of the list is this inconvenient word, "factions." This statement about not inheriting the kingdom is not a distant, eternal statement. It's a statement about the here and now. It's a statement related to the fulfillment of the "Thy Kingdom Come" prayer.

In the same way, Jesus, in John 17 communicates the need for and effect of unity in the Body. There is something supernatural in the unity of the global Church. It speaks a message of the divinity of Christ. It is the vehicle through which God desires to manifest His kingdom. And right here, in Galatians 5, we see those who live factioned lives will not inherit the kingdom.

God's heart for the Church is unity. Jesus prayed it for us. Acts demonstrated it. Paul warned us of those who would seek to de-

SPIRITUAL INNOVATION

stroy it. And the generation alive today can see it come to fruition as we love that which God loves—His Church—and unite under one head—Christ.

You have an incredibly integral role in manifesting the kingdom of heaven on earth. But the job is far too large for you to do it alone. And it's far too vast for us to try and accomplish the task divided.

No, as we increase in intimacy with God, He will continue to give us a vision for what the Church is and will be. He will continue to move us, not further apart, but closer together. There will be tensions, difficulties, balances, and compromises. But like our faith, we must hold our structures and systems loosely because what we see, practice, and believe today is only the beginning of what God wants us to step into so that we might accomplish the task of reconciling all creation back to Him.

A GLIMPSE OF A BETTER REALITY

As we step into deeper life with God individually, and as the Church is refined to become a unified body manifesting kingdom culture, the world around us will also be changed.

One small glimpse of changed culture is Walt Disney's dream for what he wanted to accomplish in Florida. I've talked about Disney World several times throughout this book. I've also talked about the creativity and imagination that exists in bringing the stories of our childhood into three dimensional life. But what most people don't know about Walt Disney World is that what it has become is only a small fraction of what Walt Disney himself hoped it would some day be. Disney World was never meant to be an amusement park in its fully realized state.

Before his death, Walt Disney taped a documentary on something he called EPCOT : Experimental Prototype Community of Tomorrow. It was a major metropolitan city, built upon innovation. It wasn't a theme park. It wasn't a facade. It wasn't the Stepford Wives or the Truman Show. It wasn't a whitewashed, planned community. It was a real vision for a real community in which people would live, work and play. It was a city with innovation at its core, a model for all a city could be.

In EPCOT's center would be leading companies from all over the world. Their research and development would take place in this city center, full of high rises designed by the world's leading architects. Around the city center would be "World Showcase"—a year-round World's Fair in which people would shop, dine, and find the world's best entertainment. There would be no vehicles in the city center. All supplies and materials for this downtown area would be delivered via underground roadway tunnels.

Around EPCOT's city center would be large expanses of green space, in which residents would relax and play. And on the outside of the green space would be suburban neighborhoods. But not just any neighborhoods. Neighborhoods of innovation, you might call them. Residents might come home one afternoon to find a new appliance installed by General Electric—something just recently developed in their R&D facilities downtown. EPCOT was a collaborative environment where not only the companies anticipated innovation, but the residents participated in testing it, providing feedback and helping build a better product.

And no need for a car. Residents and visitors would travel between the suburban neighborhoods and the downtown metropolis via electromagnetically powered, silent vehicles. Prototypes of these vehicles were tested and still exist in both Disneyland and at the Magic Kingdom. In fact, when on the TomorrowLand Transit Authority ride at the Magic Kingdom in Orlando, you can see part of the original model of Disney's EPCOT—the only vestige of a grand idea about

SPIRITUAL INNOVATION

what could have been. It was a glimpse of how humanity could live and work together, always with an expectation of innovation and forward movement.

One of the things I love about Walt Disney's vision was that it wasn't birthed out of some idealistic bubble. Walt Disney was well aware of the horrors of the second world war—albeit from state side. He was a member of an anti-communist group in Hollywood. And Disney was dreaming during an age in which dystopian novels abounded. In fact, Disney was friends with Ray Bradbury, the author of Fahrenheit 451. But Disney's ability to dream and cast that dream for others moved even Bradbury.

"Everyone in the world will come to these gates. Why? Because they want to look at the world of the future. They want to see how to make better human beings. That's what the whole thing is about. The cynics are already here and they're terrifying one another. What Disney is doing is showing the world that there are alternative ways to do things that can make us all happy. If we can borrow some of the concepts of Disneyland and Disney World and Epcot, then indeed the world can be a better place."

Author Ray Bradbury talking about Epcot Center in the September 1982 issue of "OMNI" magazine (http://travel.usatoday.com/alliance/destinations/mouseplanet/post/2012/06/Walts-Friend-Ray-Bradbury/710900/1)

Over a decade after Walt Disney's death, Bradbury still believed in Disney's dream. Epcot Center opened in 1982—not as the city of the future but a theme park. And the ride inside the geodesic sphere—that iconic "golf ball" at the entrance to the park—was Bradbury's creation called "Spaceship Earth."

I love Disney's expectation and hope for the future and his belief that he had the ability and opportunity to shape it. It gives me reason to believe this is possible for us.

"EPCOT will take its cue from the new ideas and new technologies that are emerging from the forefront of American industry. It will be a community of tomorrow that will never be completed. It will always be showcasing and testing and demonstrating new materials and new systems." (October 27, 1966)

I am inspired by his willingness to give his entire life for the work. If EPCOT would have ever become a realized dream, I would have probably run for mayor. I won't for a second say Disney's vision was wrong or misguided. I believe his dreams reflected some of God's hopes for humanity and community and what it could look like to live in a peaceful, environmentally-friendly city, built on the belief that things can always get better.

But, what Disney envisioned was only a stepping stone. It was only the beginning of what could be. It was only a small glimpse into a giant picture. And one of the things I actually love is that this dream was birthed in the heart of someone who really didn't have all that much to do with God—at least in the traditional sense.

THE KINGDOM IN THE UNIVERSE

I love that the book of Revelation ends with a city. God doesn't, in the end, rescue us from earth. He makes all things new. He brings every idea and concept and spiritual and physical reality to completion in Christ. He establishes the new Jerusalem here on earth. In Genesis 11, the people—despite God's command to disperse throughout the earth—make plans to build a city. They begin to do so and quite effectively. God says, "If as one people speaking the same language they have begun to do this, then nothing they plan to do will be impossible for them." (v. 6) This is a declaration of human ingenuity and capability, even in those who would oppose God. But God, knowing our best is in Him, disrupted the work of Babel.

What kind of implications does this have for us?

Thousands of years later, by His grace, through the power of the Holy Spirit and in alignment with Jesus' "Thy kingdom come" prayer, God is establishing the new Jerusalem, the anti-Babel, a restored Eden. We have the Old Testament promise that there will be no end to the increase of His government; and the New Testament promise that we are being transformed from glory to glory. In light of these promises, we have the opportunity to usher in an increased measure of God's kingdom on earth. We're not spiraling toward destruction. Jesus commissioned us with the task of seeing a continual increase of His glory and kingdom on the earth, all the way through to the end. Then He empowered us to do it.

We see so many people in the pages of the Old Testament accomplishing such powerful things—before the coming of Christ, before the infilling of the Holy Spirit. We see so many people in the course of human history, innovating and developing and dreaming and helping the earth resemble a little more of the kingdom of heaven every day—a majority of them not in a relationship with Jesus. The reality of the situation is that the world is progressing along pretty well without Christians. People are living longer, more healthy, more productive lives. We're eliminating disease and death. We're eliminating poverty and slavery. Peace is on the rise. And many of those things are thanks to people outside the Christian faith.

The evidence suggests that God, in His love and compassion, is committed to that which he has commissioned the Church to do. God wants peace for all people. He wants the end of sickness. He wants creation to be rescued from chaos and confusion and pain. God wants to fulfill that prayer of Jesus that has already been prayed, "Thy kingdom come. Thy will be done on earth as it is in heaven." And he's accomplishing that objective through people who will listen—even if those people don't know they're listening to Him.

But what if the people who were trying to listen to Him were also the ones who were committed to innovating? What insane things happen when those with the mind of Christ approach the natural problems of the world with supernatural power? The mind of Christ is beyond time. It's beyond human limitations. The mind of Christ makes us super-dreamers. It makes us transcendentally creative. We become exponentially imaginative. We expect beyond the scope of our own ability. And we see things happen outside the known realm of human ability and scientific understanding.

What if those filled with the Holy Spirit were to step into a place of dreaming? What if we were asking the Lord for supernatural wisdom in how to build cities and roads and schools and communities? That's what it means for the kingdom of heaven to come to earth. It's not only a metaphysical manifestation, it's a practical one—in every area of life.

MANNA MOMENTS

One of the first times I can remember encountering the concept of supernatural thinking was in Ms. Norris's sixth grade class. There are three things I remember about Ms. Norris. 1.) She wanted to be cremated. 2.) She graduated from college on 6/6/66. And 3.) She was the first person to introduce me to Madeleine L'Engle through her book, *A Wrinkle In Time*. [Sidebar: in case you haven't picked up on it yet, I think I have a crush on the now deceased L'Engle. I imagine, had she been born in a different time and place, we would have been married. She was one of the only people about whom, upon hearing of her death, I've ever thought, "Golly. I'm really sad I never got to meet her." Now to the point.]

A Wrinkle In Time is a book about the multi-dimensional travel of some children in search of their father. At one point, they find themselves on a planet inhabited by eyeless creatures. To them, the concept of sight is incomprehensible. Here's a conversation between Meg and Aunt Beast.

"Why is it so dark in here?" Meg asked. She tried to look around, but all she could see was shadows. Nevertheless there was a sense of openness, a feel of a gentle breeze moving lightly about, that kept the darkness from being oppressive.

Perplexity came to her from the beast. "What is this dark? What is this light? We do not understand. Your father and the boy, Calvin, have asked this, too. They say that it is now night on our planet, and that they cannot see. They have told us that our atmosphere is what they call opaque, so that the stars are not visible, and then they were surprised that we know stars, that we know their music and the movements of their dance far better than beings like you who spend hours studying them through what you call telescopes. We do not understand what this means, to see."

"Well, it's what things look like," Meg said helplessly.

"We do not know what things look like, as you say," the beast said. "We know what things are like. It must be a very limiting things, this seeing." ... "Later on you must try to explain some more to me."

"All right," Meg promised, and yet she knew that to try to explain anything that could be seen with the eyes would be impossible, because the beasts in some way saw, knew, understood, far more completely than she...

What a beautiful description of what it means to walk by faith, not by sight! It's a beautiful picture of living a life based not on our own understanding but, in all our ways acknowledging Him. This type of depth and experience and understanding is what it means to live, not with human wisdom, but with spiritual wisdom.

Scripture talks a lot about the difference between earthly and spiritual wisdom. Earthly wisdom answers our questions by satiating our curiosity—thus puffing us up as informed and "right." Spiritual wisdom brings deeper revelation and helps us discover how little we know. It makes us more curious. It causes us to pursue, to press in deeper. Spiritual wisdom doesn't answer our questions. It causes us to ask more. It widens our paradigm. It blows our minds.

How often did people walk away from a conversation with Jesus with all their questions answered? Rather, he would often cause people to look deeper or broader or through different eyes altogether. The religious were dumbfounded and silenced while the seekers walked away in awe, asking more questions.

1 Corinthians 2:12-13 illuminates this deeper reality for us. In Christ, we are not limited to, nor constrained by, the limitations of human thinking. Rather, we have something more.

What we have received is not the spirit of the world, but the Spirit who is from God, so that we may understand what God has freely given us. This is what we speak, not in words taught us by human wisdom but in words taught by the Spirit, explaining spiritual realities with Spirit-taught words.

We have a different vocabulary, a different source of wisdom and thinking. We don't simply think from the outside in, taking in data and interpreting it with the head and heart. We, in Christ, have the ability to reason from the inside out. As the Holy Spirit fills us, we have the ability to offer words, thoughts, solutions that confound even the wise of this world.

If we lean into this truth, I think we'll be amazed by the way God supernaturally provides.

When the Israelites were moving through the desert, they were hungry and without food. God decided to make supernatural provision for them in what we traditionally know as "manna." He did so by covering the ground with a layer of dew, and as it dried, the dew turned to bread. But manna isn't a random collection of sounds. Manna sounds like the Hebrew words for "what is it?" God provided this heavenly bread, in a supernatural way, and the response of the people was, "What is it?" It was beyond their realm of comprehension, delivered in a way that was unknown and unexpected. It was such a surprising, gracious gift that all the Hebrews could say was, "What is it?"

I believe God wants to use you and the Church for an unlimited number of "what is it?" moments. God's heart is that, through His Church, His manifold, multifaceted, unlimited, amazing wisdom would be unleashed upon the earth. And as the world encounters these revelations of His power, character, and activity, they will say, "what is it?"

Certain pockets of the Church love to talk about evangelism. Others avoid it altogether. But the Evangelical view of evangelism is based on a battle of the wits—a process of convincing.

Throughout the New Testament, we have example after example of people following Jesus as the result of "manna" moments ("What is it?"). Jesus would perform miracles and the question people would end up asking was, "Who is this man?!" The New Testament saints, following in Jesus footsteps, doing greater things than even Jesus did, would perform miracles and people would ask, "By what authority, by whose name do you do these things?" The New Testament model of evangelism is often accompanied by supernatural activity. It wasn't the process of winning an argument. It was a supernatural work that came by supernatural means.

No one comes to Jesus unless the Father draws him. And when God shows up, God shows up big. God brings people to awe, asking,

"What is it?"

These types of things take risk. When Elijah encountered the 450 prophets of Baal and the 400 prophets of Asherah on Mount Carmel, everything about it was a risk. And Elijah made the decision to make it even riskier. Not only did he challenge the prophets. He told them to cover the altar with jug after jug of water. He wanted to do everything he could to make sure no one thought it was a trick. Elijah wanted everyone to see the consuming power of God that day. And when he called down the power of God, God came. That day, the people turned back to God.

The book of James says Elijah was a man just like us. Jesus said that we would do the miracles we have seen him do and even greater things. These stories we read in the Bible aren't distant realities for us. Neither are they things to be simply replicated by you and me. No. They are the foundation for what's to come. They are only the beginning of the fullness of what God wants to accomplish.

You haven't been placed here on this earth to be part of an impotent religion. You are here because it was God's pleasure to create you. He created you to live a risky life full of stories worth telling. That means releasing control and expecting to live in the miraculous.

God wants to use you to bring about things that have yet to exist. God wants to use you as a vessel for a greater revelation of Himself and His kingdom. You are an agent of Spiritual Innovation. Expect huge things. Expect God to show up in the most supernatural and practical of ways—in your life, in your relationships, in your work and in your passions. You have the power to change the world here and now. Go do it.

SPIRITUAL INNOVATION

QUESTIONS AND CONVERSATIONS:

- How are you living a life that fosters Spiritual Innovation? Do you give time to cultivating intimacy with God? How? Are you living with an expectation of what the universe could look like in the context of heaven coming to earth? What does that look like?

- Do you see your role in bringing the kingdom as part of a greater whole? In what ways are you joining with other people in order to see heaven come to earth? How can you grow in your partnership and collaboration with others?

- How are you cultivating a life of manna moments by living beyond the limits of your human capacity? How can you move forward in this into a greater level of Spiritual Innovation?

DO SOMETHING:

This is the final "do something" in the book. It's a call to be a spiritual innovator. It's a challenge to live life with a greater level of expectation of what's possible. It's a vision for a different world and a recognition that the mission of heaven on earth comes through you. Practice the power you have as a result of the infilling of the Holy Spirit to be an agent of change everywhere you go. Now, go dream big and expect God to exceed your dreams.

SPIRITUAL INNOVATION // AN AFTERWARD
HONOR AND EXCEED

SPIRITUAL INNOVATION

Throughout this book, I've given some things a hard time. I've discussed what I perceive to be some of the shortcomings of the current state of Evangelicalism in America. I've talked about the Protestant Reformation and questioned its helpfulness to the Church as a whole. I've asked some questions related to some tightly held doctrines. But at the end of the day, I want to end this book with these two words: Honor and Exceed.

We, as a Church, must honor those who have come before us and recognize the contributions they have made to us and the advancement of the kingdom. It's easy to paint with broad brush strokes, but there's no brush broad enough and fine enough to paint the full picture of billions of people who have come before us, setting the stage for what we will do now. Let us remember the many wonderful things we've learned from our parents' generation. Let us acknowledge and celebrate where we are today. Remember how they—with sincerity and love—so often desired to raise us with a knowledge of Christ. Let us honor the last 50 years of American Evangelicalism that, while not perfectly executed, wanted the world to know God.

And that second word: Exceed. Expect it. Pray for it. Desire it. Expect to be exceeded. Hold lightly to your systems and methodologies. Because we are, in fact, only one generation in a process thousands of years in the making. We, like the generations who have come before us, have not seen a completed revelation of the kingdom of heaven on earth. And until that day, let us pray for it. Let us raise up the coming generation to believe that they can bring more of it.

Paul, in his letter to the Ephesians, says, we are "built on the foundation of the apostles and prophets, with Christ Jesus himself as the chief cornerstone." It's a recognition that those who have come before us have played a role in who we are today. We must honor that. He then goes on to say, "In him the whole building is joined together and rises to become a holy temple in the Lord. And in him you too are being built together to become a dwelling in which God lives by his Spirit." We are joined together with those who have come before us to be the dwelling place of God. (Ephesians 2:20-22)

Rebellion is the posture of a generation that follows a generation afraid of being exceeded. God has built something into our very nature that desires change and growth. When a generation is raised to believe the best they can be is to be exactly like the people who came before them, the only choice they have is rebellion. In these cases, rebellion, although difficult, is necessary. But when a generation is platformed, they move forward, not in rebellion, but in an accelerated state of thriving. Their growth is not like that of a plant whose roots are bound by a pot and whose leaves are hidden from the sun. Rather they are like a plant well-cultivated and fertilized.

The Church—with the exception of some pockets of revival—has seen a steady decline in the work and power of the Holy Spirit since the miraculous state of the Church as recorded in Acts. You and I have stepped into a process 1900 years in the making. And the beautiful part of all of it is—we can be the turning point. The generation alive today, the people reading this book, can be a generation that changes the game. We can be the people who turn the corner to see an empowered Church, through whom a greater revelation of the character of God and His kingdom are made manifest on the earth.

We can pray and expect God will take back the years the enemy has stolen. We can expect and hope for a re-unified Church. We can expect, in our lifetime, the end of the Catholic, Protestant divide. We can pray for the end of denominational division. We can call one another to the end of factions—a condition Paul points out will prevent us from inheriting the kingdom (Galatians 5:19-21). We can expect to be a people who, once again, hear the voice of God as clearly as the prophets of old.

We can be people who, like Jesus, see and hear the Father and do what He's doing and say what He's saying.

Lord Jesus, as we see these things come in our lifetime, even if we don't see the full coming of them, we expect to be exceeded by those who come after us. We will not box you in. We will not succumb to the lie that our understanding of you is the full revelation of who you are. Instead, we will soak in as much of you that you allow us to see.

Lord, we will raise our children to exceed us. We will train and encourage them to be a generation who sees your face and hears your voice. We will continually remind them they are here to see a more complete revelation of "Thy kingdom come!" We will platform them to be a generation of healing, wholeness, blessing, peace, and love. God, we ask for a great coming of yourself and your kingdom as we anticipate—by your Spirit and on the rock of Christ—a new level of Spiritual Innovation.

www.ingramcontent.com/pod-product-compliance
Lightning Source LLC
Chambersburg PA
CBHW071213090426
42736CB00014B/2798